China's Strong Arm
Protecting Citizens and Assets Abroad

Jonas Parello-Plesner

and Mathieu Duchâtel

China's Strong Arm
Protecting Citizens and Assets Abroad

Jonas Parello-Plesner

and Mathieu Duchâtel

IISS The International Institute for Strategic Studies

The International Institute for Strategic Studies

Arundel House I 13–15 Arundel Street I Temple Place I London I WC2R 3DX I UK

First published May 2015 **Routledge**
4 Park Square, Milton Park, Abingdon, Oxon, OX14 4RN

for **The International Institute for Strategic Studies**
Arundel House, 13–15 Arundel Street, Temple Place, London, WC2R 3DX, UK
www.iiss.org

Simultaneously published in the USA and Canada by **Routledge**
270 Madison Ave., New York, NY 10016

Routledge is an imprint of Taylor & Francis, an Informa Business

DIRECTOR-GENERAL AND CHIEF EXECUTIVE Dr John Chipman
EDITOR Dr Nicholas Redman
EDITORIAL MANAGER Nancy Turner
ASSISTANT EDITOR Sarah Johnstone
EDITORIAL Jill Lally, Chris Raggett
COVER/PRODUCTION John Buck, Kelly Verity
COVER IMAGE Getty

The International Institute for Strategic Studies is an independent centre for research, information and debate on the problems of conflict, however caused, that have, or potentially have, an important military content. The Council and Staff of the Institute are international and its membership is drawn from almost 100 countries. The Institute is independent and it alone decides what activities to conduct. It owes no allegiance to any government, any group of governments or any political or other organisation. The IISS stresses rigorous research with a forward-looking policy orientation and places particular emphasis on bringing new perspectives to the strategic debate.

The Institute's publications are designed to meet the needs of a wider audience than its own membership and are available on subscription, by mail order and in good bookshops. Further details at www.iiss.org.

Printed and bound in Great Britain by Bell & Bain Ltd, Thornliebank, Glasgow

British Library Cataloguing in Publication Data
A catalogue record for this book is available from the British Library

Library of Congress Cataloging in Publication Data

ADELPHI series
ISSN 1944-5571

ADELPHI 451
ISBN 978-1-138-94726-9

Contents

ACKNOWLEDGEMENTS

This book was initially discussed during a talk in 2013 with Adam Ward and Nigel Inkster from IISS. Thanks to both for believing in the idea of what was at that time called 'China's Great Power Burden' and for suggesting it for an Adelphi publication.

Since then we have been in editor Nick Redman's capable hands who has steered us successfully to completion of the book. Particular and well-deserved thanks for the editing process goes to Sarah Johnstone who came on board in the final phase but who diligently took upon her to polish our rough edges and probe all our sources until the very last minute including spending her entire birthday this year on our book.

Jonas would like to thank former colleagues – particularly Mark Leonard and Francois Godement – at the think tank European Council on Foreign Relation from 2010 to 2013 for a high-powered intellectual environment discussing the possible trajectories of China's rise. Also thanks to Hans Kundnani for alerting me to the historical parallels of the Don Pacifico affair in protecting nationals. Thanks to Ger Wang for assisting Jonas on finding sources in the Libya, Mekong and Sudan chapters. You deserve much more than a lunch at Capitol Grille (all you asked for).

A big thanks to my family, Kristin, Felix and Victor for continued endurance and patience with a dad/husband running between a full time day job and writing in the weekends. It wasn't always fun and as 11-year old Victor often said, 'how long can it take to write a book?' Too long, but now it is done.

Thanks to Andrew Small for insightful comments on the Afghanistan-Pakistan chapter. Thanks to Yun Sun at the Stimson Center for letting us borrow some of her Chinese language books on the Libya-evacuation. Thanks to Zhou Hang for comments on the Sudan chapter and letting us benefit from his own research from his time at SIPRI. Thanks to the many Chinese officials, who always prefer to stay anonymous, and academics who have been discussing with us over the years how China protects nationals abroad. All errors or omissions in the book rest with us.

GLOSSARY

CHINCA	China International Contractors Association
CCC	China Communications Construction
CNPC	China National Petroleum Corporation
COSCO	China Ocean Shipping Company
CSCEC	China State Construction Engineering Group
JCC	Jiangxi Copper Corporation
JEM	Justice and Equality Movement
MCC	Metallurgical Corporation of China
MFA	Ministry of Foreign Affairs
MOFCOM	Ministry of Commerce
MPS	Ministry of Public Security
NDRC	National Development and Reform Commission
OECD	Organisation for Economic Co-operation and Development
SASAC	State-owned Assets Supervision and Administration Commission (of the State Council)
SLM	Sudan Liberation Movement
SOEs	State-owned enterprises
SPLM	Sudan People's Liberation Movement
UNAMID	African Union/United Nations Hybrid operation in Darfur
UNMISS	United Nations Mission in South Sudan

INTRODUCTION

In March 2015, two Chinese frigates, the *Linyu* and *Weifang*, evacuated 629 Chinese citizens and 279 other foreign nationals from war-torn Yemen. This was a historic move for China, since it was the first time that the People's Liberation Army (PLA) Navy had conducted such a non-combatant evacuation operation alone, and one of the first times that China had rescued other foreign nationals. It demonstrated China's growing capacity to protect its nationals in faraway places. Indeed, China's ambassador to Yemen, Tian Qi, told Xinhua that the *Noah's Ark* evacuation 'reflected a significant growth in China's comprehensive national power'.[1]

China's increasing desire and capacity to protect nationals and assets abroad, and its effect on Chinese foreign policy, is the leitmotif of this book. China is increasingly compelled to protect a growing number of citizens abroad. As Chinese business has expanded across the world, so the Chinese government has had to cope with a new map of global risks for its overseas interests. Traditionally constrained by the long-standing principle of 'non-interference' in other states' affairs, Chinese foreign policy has had to adapt.

Successive crises since the mid-2000s have already transformed Chinese behaviour in emergency situations. Similar events in the future will continue to shape China's approach to international intervention and power projection, with the protection of nationals overseas a major driver of foreign-policy change. At a time when the attention of the global strategic community is on China's maritime behaviour in Asia, and when 'assertive' has become a common description of Chinese foreign policy under President Xi Jinping, it is worth understanding this other significant area of change, with its equally far-reaching consequences for the future of China as a great power and international-security actor.

Securing Chinese interests abroad in times of crisis will puncture any notion of an entirely frictionless expansion of Chinese business and human presence around the globe. China is already in the top tier of foreign investors, with overseas investments worth US$101 billion in 2013 and growing at more than US$10bn a year.[2] Chinese companies are in hot pursuit of oil and natural resources abroad, particularly in Africa. China has left few regions of the world unexplored, and is now promoting the construction of a 'New Silk Road' from Asia to foreign markets in Europe and eastern Africa.

Such global expansion has led to growing numbers of Chinese workers and other citizens overseas. Many of the decisions to venture abroad have demonstrated a high appetite for risk. In the energy sector, Chinese companies have invested in markets off limits to their Western counterparts because of sanctions or avoided by Western firms because of the extreme danger involved, including Sudan and South Sudan. A similar picture emerges in mining and construction, with Chinese companies engaged in such danger spots as Afghanistan and Libya. This expansion into areas where there is a lack of Western competition and the search for high investment returns explains the high tolerance to security risk.

This global presence leads to a new risk map for China, in which Chinese companies have been attacked, and Chinese citizens killed, wounded or kidnapped on several continents (see map, pp. 28–29). Non-combatant evacuations have also become standard practice in crises overseas; China has conducted 17 of these in the past decade. In 2011, China rescued more than 47,000 Chinese abroad, more in a single year than in the previous decades of the People's Republic. On the one hand, evacuations are an easy way out of conflict and fit China's traditional reluctance to get heavily engaged in crisis management or resolution. On the other hand, the mass evacuation from Libya in 2011 and the smaller rescue from Yemen in 2015 show that civilian agencies are not the only instruments of government policy in the overseas protection of nationals – and that the People's Liberation Army and PLA Navy also take a leading role. This raises new questions about future Chinese power projection and Chinese moves to protect overseas interests during international crises.

To a large degree, China is 'looking inwards' to meet this new challenge. Government agencies and firms are building capacity and establishing standard operating procedures to reduce risks and manage crises. Different government ministries and other institutions each have different roles to play, and each is adapting accordingly, trying to learn from past mistakes to improve its performance in future. This gradual adaptation of Chinese foreign-policy actors is occurring in response to unforeseen and often unpredictable events.

Inflection points for Chinese foreign policy

The extent of change in China's foreign policy, and the variety of responses, has so far depended on the nature of the specific crisis. However, all indicators point to greater Chinese involvement abroad. China has been accused of 'free-riding' on the NATO-led military intervention in Afghanistan, with Chinese companies making investments in the war-torn country and hoping to benefit from the improved security that international troops would bring, without China's having to undertake much effort in fostering stability and security. At the same time, Afghanistan and neighbouring Pakistan have posed a tremendous challenge to Chinese safety, not only because of the many attacks on Chinese citizens in these two countries, but also because of the risk that terrorism there could spill over into Xinjiang province and the rest of China, or affect Chinese interests in Central Asian countries. Chinese analysts have worried about this explosive potential for years.

China has shown its usual inclination to work directly with host governments and demand assurances for the protection of Chinese interests in Afghanistan and Pakistan. However, as China has tried to find a balance between effectively protecting Chinese nationals and securing itself against terrorist spillover into Xinjiang, on the one hand, and supporting strategic trade and investment in the neighbourhood, on the other hand, there have been reports of Chinese officials making contact with Taliban groups. The growing threat of terrorism to China and Chinese nationals is likely to be another pull factor persuading Chinese authorities, particularly the country's security apparatus, to venture overseas. The case of China in Afghanistan and Pakistan during the past decade highlights a pattern of gradual foreign-policy adjustment, closely linked to the protection of nationals overseas.

In Libya, China demonstrated to its domestic audience and to the wider world that it was capable of lifting its citizens, en masse, out of harm's way. In 12 days in late February and early March 2011, China removed more than 35,000 workers by plane, ship, bus and truck from the turmoil of a nascent uprising against the regime of Muammar Gadhafi. The evacuation was the largest in China's history, and the first to involve military planes in airlifting civilians to safety. While Chinese companies suffered economic losses as a result of this sudden evacuation, the Chinese government gained in reputation. The action it took suggests there could be similar contingencies in future when civilian planes and ferry boats would not suffice for a safe and orderly exodus. Libya also broke new ground for China in being the first time it voted in the UN Security Council to sanction the authoritarian Gadhafi for mistreatment of his population, and acquiesced to a second resolution that eventually led to regime change.

Later that year, events on the Mekong River underlined the difficulty of adhering to the principle of non-interference when protecting nationals abroad. As a response to the brutal murders of 13 Chinese sailors in an apparent drug-trafficking case, Chinese law officials contemplated using a drone to strike the Burmese drug kingpin, and chief suspect, Naw Kham. Instead, after a protracted manhunt in cooperation with local police, Chinese law enforcement extradited Naw Kham and put him on trial in Kunming, before delivering a death sentence and eventually executing him. Faced with ever-growing calls from the Chinese public to track down the perpetrators and bring them to justice, Beijing found itself inexorably pulled into deeper involvement in its neighbourhood, despite its hands-off foreign policy. The Mekong case also saw the Ministry of Public Security (MPS) take a more prominent foreign-policy role. Under the leadership of the then-powerful Zhou Yongkang, the MPS used security risks to Chinese nationals overseas to support the internationalisation of its law-enforcement activities, not only in China's neighbourhood but also in some African countries.

China has long made it a point of policy to talk only with 'legitimate' state actors, but one of the key ways its foreign policy has changed has been its engagement with a wider range of interlocutors. This has happened in Afghanistan, Pakistan and Libya. However, nowhere has this evolution been more far-reaching than in the Sudans, where Chinese state-owned companies ventured exclusively for oil but subsequently, with the rest of the Chinese government, had to deal with attacks on Chinese nationals and unwanted foreign-policy conundrums such as South Sudanese independence. The commercial and human presence gradually led to a more proactive Chinese approach to securing national interests. This has now extended to the fielding of Chinese combat troops as part of a United Nations mission. China has long been a major contributor to peacekeeping operations but had until very recently refrained from dispatching combat units.

Responsibility to protect points to further foreign-policy change

Through a process of accretion, therefore, China can be said to have adopted a responsibility to protect its own citizens overseas. The concept of 'protecting nationals abroad' (*haiwai gongmin baohu*) was added to the Communist Party's priority list at the 18th Party Congress in 2012, as President Xi and new Premier Li Keqiang assumed control of the Chinese government and military apparatus. In 2013, the White Paper on Defence mentioned the protection of nationals and interests overseas for the first time, and defined providing reliable security support for China's interests overseas as one of the PLA's missions.

The globalisation of Chinese interests has paved the way in the past decade for a gradual redefinition of China's non-interference principle, but more dramatic events could lead China

into an even greater shift. A decade ago, few would have coun-
tenanced the idea of China sending naval ships into distant
waters. This would have been seen as violating the 'non-interference' principle. Yet from 2008 onwards, Beijing did indeed
deploy frigates in the Gulf of Aden to protect merchant ships
and Chinese sailors from Somali pirates. The same flotilla was
later involved in evacuations from Libya and Yemen. While the
old maxim says 'trade follows the flag', the Chinese position
is today reversed: as Chinese commercial interests and human
presence expand, the apparatus of the Chinese state is forced to
follow suit. There are historical precedents for this, of course,
including during the days of British Empire when adventurous
British nationals often compelled the Crown to follow them
into unknown territory.

Despite these developments, one should always bear in
mind that engagement in other countries' affairs doesn't come
naturally to China. Non-interference remains deeply ingrained
in the Chinese government's DNA and foreign-policy scrip-
tures – as does paramount leader Deng Xiaoping's dictum
about 'keeping a low profile'. Chinese foreign policy is habitu-
ally hands-off, with little ambition to shape the international
security environment, despite the fact that China is one of
the five permanent members of the United Nations Security
Council.

Instead, the overriding government priority in recent decades
has been economic progress in China facilitated by trade and
investment with the rest of the world. To this end, foreign policy
has been designed to ensure that China's global business runs
smoothly. The notion of the country's 'peaceful rise' or 'peaceful development', coined by top political adviser Zheng Bijian in
2003, insists that China's growth is both peaceful and economi-
cally beneficial to the rest of the world. The concept was crafted
as a retort to the 'China threat theory' that posits that the rise of

China as a great power will necessarily lead to military conflict. Xi Jinping's 'China Dream' continues that 'peaceful rise' thinking, albeit with more nationalistic undertones.[3]

The question of which road to great-power status China will take is going to fuel debate both in and outside China for some years to come. The protection of Chinese nationals overseas is a question of a different nature, but with equally large ramifications for China as a great power. It is about China's adaptation to new international challenges, and ongoing domestic reform and change within government agencies, enterprises and the military.

In becoming more deeply involved on the world stage, China has mainly reacted to events on the ground, rather than seizing opportunities to expand its political influence and power globally. It has never shied away from experimenting with pragmatic solutions, but the ad hoc nature of the shift in Chinese behaviour means it defies analysis focused on grand strategy. It appears that China's power projection is being pulled along by a vague notion that lives must be protected when security somewhere abroad seriously deteriorates. Optimists will argue that this incorporation of humanitarian norms into Chinese foreign policy is to be welcomed and supported. Pessimists will see nationalistic overtones and anticipate the overseas deployment of Chinese military forces in coming decades for narrow national interests.

Protecting Chinese nationals abroad is impossible with a hands-off approach. There are many signs that the Chinese government would prefer to continue doing business globally without strategic involvement, but this era of frictionless expansion – if it ever really existed – is definitely over. Confronted by new global risks, Chinese foreign policy needs to find new ways to prevent and manage crises, while projecting power and influence.

The course China chooses to achieve this will matter enormously for its relations with Western and other states. The government's increasing willingness to shoulder responsibility for protecting Chinese overseas interests might not make China the 'responsible stakeholder' in world affairs that the United States in particular covets. However, it will mean a China more actively looking out for its own interests in situations of upheaval; sometimes, as in South Sudan where China has sent peacekeepers, these may even align with Western concerns. Studying China's new 'risk map', as outlined in this book, offers indications of how China may continue to behave on its path to great-power status.

Notes

1 'Chinese naval vessels evacuate hundreds from war-torn Yemen', Xinhua, 8 April 2015.

2 'World Investment Report: Annex Tables', United Nations Conference on Trade and Development (UNCTAD), accessed at http://unctad.org/en/pages/DIAE/World%20Investment%20Report/Annex-Tables.aspx.

3 For more on the China Dream, see 'Chinese Dream', Xinhua, accessed at http://www.xinhuanet.com/english/special/chinesedream/. A quick précis is found at 'What does Xi Jinping's China Dream mean?', BBC News, 6 June 2013.

CHAPTER ONE

China's new global risk map

China's search for business opportunities abroad has meant it is gradually becoming more entangled in a messy geopolitical world. When the Chinese Communist Party officially endorsed the 'going-out policy' in 2002 to encourage Chinese companies to invest overseas, the magnitude of the decision might not have been fully appreciated.[1] More than a dozen years later, the strategic decision to support the international expansion of Chinese business has already reshaped the country's threat perceptions and security interests. China is now a major-league foreign investor, with outward foreign direct investment (FDI) reaching a record high of US$101 billion in 2013 – up more than 15% year on year.[2] In the first half of 2014, the Organisation for Economic Cooperation and Development estimated that China was among the top five overseas investors.[3]

China's new global footprint exposes Chinese companies to greater threats, and the Chinese government has in many ways been compelled to 'go global' to protect these new-found interests abroad. Never before has geopolitical risk and conflict overseas so impacted Chinese economic and security interests. But it is not only Chinese companies globalising; the fate and well-being of millions of Chinese individuals abroad has, via intense media and public scrutiny, also become part of the Chinese national interest. Estimates put the number of Chinese nationals overseas at more than 5 million, including up to 2m in Africa – although, as with most other aspects of China's rise, available numbers are not always accurate and many statistics are simply not collected or published by government agencies and firms. Chinese expatriate workers are exposed to the risk of terrorist attacks, kidnappings and local unrest. In the past few years alone, they have been caught up in civil wars in Libya, Syria, Sudan, the Central African Republic and Iraq. Our collected data suggest that 100 or more Chinese nationals have died abroad in the past decade as a result of geopolitical violence. Thousands more are under threat. Future uncertainties demand new types of risk management by Chinese companies and the state.

Chinese economic expansion abroad

China's global footprint expands through what appear in Ministry of Commerce (MOFCOM) statistics as 'contracted projects overseas', mostly infrastructure contracts signed by Chinese construction firms with foreign governments. According to MOFCOM, the value of new contracts signed in 2013 was US$171.6bn.[4] Many of these investments and contracts are in labour-intensive sectors, not only in construction but also in the extraction of energy and mineral resources.

State-owned enterprises (SOEs) are driving the global expansion of Chinese direct investment. In 2010, FDI by SOEs accounted for 61.6% of outward flows, while the stock of foreign investment controlled by SOEs accounted for 66.2% of the national total.[5] Liao Shuping, an analyst with Bank of China, notes that SOEs have greater financial resources than most private firms and enjoy 'a privileged position in terms

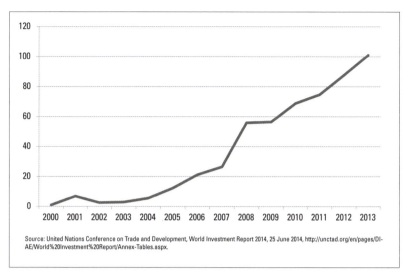

Source: United Nations Conference on Trade and Development, World Investment Report 2014, 25 June 2014, http://unctad.org/en/pages/DI-AE/World%20Investment%20Report/Annex-Tables.aspx.

Fig 1. **China's Foreign Direct Investment (US$ bn)**

of finance, taxation, employment, regulation, and investment approval'.[6] This is particularly true of the 117 'central SOEs' under the State-owned Assets Supervision and Administration Commission (SASAC) of the State Council. However, some local SOEs under the supervision of provincial SASACs have also become major international players. In 2011, SOEs represented 80% of the value of China's stock market, and consequently dominate the domestic market as well as the sphere of international expansion.[7]

SOEs are also China's most powerful actors in energy and mineral extraction, two labour-intensive sectors on which China's economic-growth aspirations depend and where scale matters enormously. In the oil sector, according to the International Energy Agency, Chinese SOEs invested US$73bn in upstream merger and acquisition deals between 2011 and 2013, compared to US$83.2bn between 2002 and 2010.[8] The list in Table 1 shows that China's three oil majors – Sinopec, CNPC and CNOOC – are also the three largest Chinese companies by FDI. The oil majors have been seeking opportunities

Table 1: **List of Chinese companies by non-financial FDI (2012)**

Rank	Company name (English)
1	China Petroleum and Chemical Corporation (Sinopec)
2	China National Petroleum Corporation (CNPC)
3	China National Offshore Oil Corporation (CNOOC)
4	China Mobile (CMCC)
5	China Resources (Holdings)
6	China Ocean Shipping Group Company (COSCO)
7	Chalco (Aluminium Corporation of China)
8	Sinochem Group
9	China Merchants Group
10	China State Construction Engineering Corporation (CSCEC)

Source: MOFCOM, '2012 nian Zhongguo feijinrong lei kuaguo gongsi 100 qiang' (The 100 largest Chinese companies in 2012 by non-financial FDI) accessed at http://images.mofcom.gov.cn/hzs/201309/20130913152843102.pdf. Although MOFCOM ranks corporations by non-financial FDI, it does not quantify their investments.

in countries where there is less international competition, such as Sudan, Syria, Libya, Myanmar and Iran. Several of these countries are considered to be fragile or rogue states, and these engagements entail new foreign-policy conundrums for the risk-averse Chinese government. This has led some Chinese scholars to criticise the oil majors for 'hijacking Chinese foreign policy'.[9]

In the mineral sector, China's footprint has enlarged to such an extent in the past decade that it is a market mover on most minerals, such as iron, lead ore, copper and nickel. For example, in 2013 China accounted for 63% of global imports of iron ore, diversifying away from its traditional suppliers (Brazil and Australia) into new projects in Africa, especially Sierra Leone, Tanzania, Zambia, Swaziland and Mozambique.[10] Central SOEs such as China Minmetals Corporation, the Metallurgical Corporation of China (MCC, which is active in Afghanistan, see Chapter Three), or provincial SOEs such as Tianjin Minerals and Equipment Group, have become important global players.

The pattern of labour-intensive economic presence also applies to infrastructure construction, a sector in which Chinese SOEs have secured numerous international contracts. Sixty Chinese companies are among the top 250 international contractors in the infrastructure sector; and an overwhelming majority of these are SOEs, most of them registered with provincial governments.[11] However, the three top players are centrally administered SOEs. The largest, China State Construction Engineering Corporation (CSCEC), claimed total revenues of US$77.2bn from overseas operations at the end of 2011. CSCEC builds airports, housing, roads, bridges, water-industry and medical-treatment facilities, hotels, government buildings, and arts and sporting facilities.[12] The second largest, China Railway Engineering Corporation (CREC), announced overseas revenues of US$3.7bn in 2013, a number it aims to triple by 2016.[13] CREC's ambition is to sell the Chinese high-speed train system in countries such as Brazil and Kazakhstan. Infrastructure construction has become a diplomatic tool, with China supporting projects via large loans from its two development banks, China Development Bank (CDB) and Exim Bank, and these loans in turn guaranteeing access to natural resources. CDB has a higher volume of loans than the World Bank, while a subsidiary China–Africa Development Fund secures funding for the continent's development and for Chinese companies' access to raw materials.[14]

In one of the most widely discussed of these agreements, the so-called 'deal of the century', China Railway Group and Sinohydro were to construct a network of transportation, mining and energy infrastructures in the Democratic Republic of the Congo (DRC) for access to cobalt and copper deposits, for a total value estimated at US$9bn at the time of signing in 2007.[15] Table 2 shows the high concentration of infrastructure in China's overseas contracts – roads, railways, harbours, dams, bridges and housing – all of which are labour-intensive undertakings. The two companies to top the ranking, Huawei and ZTE, are private telecommunications companies. Even private Chinese companies, particularly Huawei, are able to access

Table 2: **Ten largest Chinese companies by turnover of contracted projects overseas (2013)**

Rank	Company name (English)	Turnover (US$bn)
1	ZTE Corporation	13.0
2	Huawei Technologies	9.2
3	China State Construction Engineering Corporation (CSCEC)	5.7
4	Sinohydro Corporation	5.3
5	China Harbour Engineering Company (CHEC)	3.4
6	CITIC Construction	2.8
7	Shanghai Zhenhua Heavy Industries (ZPMC)	2.7
8	China Gezhouba Group Corporation (CGGC)	2.4
9	China Road and Bridge Corporation (CRBC)	2.2
10	Shandong III Electric Power Construction Corporation (SEPCO III)	2.2

Source: MOFCOM, http://www.mofcom.gov.cn/article/tongjiziliao/dgzz/201401/20140100468536.shtml.

loans from the CDB to support their international expansion.

Chinese nationals abroad

Although it is generally said that 5m Chinese passport holders reside overseas, Beijing does not have an accurate figure. Various reasons explain this lack of precise information. Primarily, government institutions have fallen behind the rapid global spread of Chinese companies and nationals. Given illegal immigration, the lack of systematic consular registration, poor formal communication between companies and the Ministry of Foreign Affairs (MFA) or MOFCOM in third countries, and the absence of accurate reporting to the government by subcontractors placing workers abroad, officials struggle to keep track of numbers. The rapid turnover of workers on international projects makes it even more difficult for consular services to capture an ever-evolving pattern of migration.

A wish to downplay the number of Chinese nationals abroad, so as to avoid a backlash in countries opening their doors to large numbers of Chinese nationals, may be another reason. As one Chinese academic explains, everyone 'downplays and under-reports real numbers for the sake of the country's image', as there is fear in China that large numbers

Table 3 **Chinese tourists go abroad in ever-larger numbers**

Year	Number of exits recorded (millions)
1997	5.3
1998	8.4
1999	9.2
2000	10.5
2001	12.1
2002	16.6
2003	20.2
2004	28.9
2005	31.0
2006	34.5
2007	40.9
2008	45.8
2009	47.7
2010	57.4
2011	70.3
2012	83.2
2013	98.2

Sources: 'Waijiaobu: 2012 nian Zhongguo neidi jumin chujing renci da 8318 wan' (MFA: In 2012, the number of Chinese nationals going abroad reached 83.18 million), *Zhongguo Wang*, 21 February 2013, accessed at http://www.ce.cn/xwzx/gnsz/gdxw/201302/21/t20130221_24131886.shtml; 'Neidi jumin quannian chujing jin yiren ci' (Number of nationals going abroad is approaching 100 million), *Fazhi Ribao*, 25 May 2014, accessed at http://www.chinanews.com/fz/2014/05-23/6203098.shtml; 'Woguo chujing you shichang de fazhan qingkuang baogao' (Analysis of the Chinese market for overseas travel), *Hongbo Report*, 24 February 2014, accessed at http://www.reporthb.com/info/infoview47166.htm.

of emigrants could harm the national image.[16] Consequently, official figures provided by the MFA, MOFCOM and the General Administration of Customs (GCA) fail to add up to the generally accepted 5m estimate. The China International Contractors Association (CHINCA) acknowledges having sent 4.9m workers abroad between 1978 and 2009.[17] (Clearly, these numbers do not include the estimated 50m 'overseas Chinese' – people of Chinese birth or descent – who hold foreign passports.).

Nevertheless, despite the lack of accurate data, Chinese government officials and experts agree that the scale of emigration is without historical precedent and is putting the consular system under great pressure. All indicators point to continuous and steady growth in the foreseeable future. This trend is reflected in the most accurate figures made public by China, namely entry/exit data provided by the GCA. Using these figures, the MFA annually reports the number of nationals travelling abroad (see Table 3). This reached 98m in 2013.[18] In the most recent years for which data are published, the number has grown at an average 10m per year. Even if these numbers do not distinguish between work-related travel, tourism, and short- and long-term departures, and include travellers to Hong Kong, Macau and Taiwan, they underline the scale of overseas travel. The MFA anticipates that this growth rate will at the very least remain stable, and most probably will accelerate. One forecast is that by 2020 some 150m Chinese will travel abroad every year.[19]

In recent years, Chinese media have consistently reported an average 800,000 Chinese working in international projects, including those funded by Chinese investment. MOFCOM collects data on the number of Chinese employees working overseas. In November 2013, the Ministry adopted new regulations to distinguish between three categories: workers (*laowu renyuan*), employees sent overseas on contracted projects (*duiwai chengbao gongcheng waipai renyuan*) and employees of foreign-investment projects (*duiwai touzi waipai renyuan*).[20] According to MOFCOM, a total 853,000 Chinese were employed abroad at the end of 2013, of which 527,000 had been sent overseas on jobs linked to Chinese investment or international contracts.[21] Official figures (see map, pp. 28–29) are much lower than the estimated sum of nationals overseas in a selection of countries where Chinese have encountered severe security risks. The figures show the key importance of contracted projects and expat workers in countries where incidents have occurred involving the safety of Chinese nationals.

Even when adding travellers to that total – and taking into account that workers are included in the customs department's travel statistics when they leave China – MOFCOM statistics do not match the estimated 5m Chinese overseas. There are also gaps in the data relating to individual countries. Examples include Angola, where MOFCOM had registered 31,905 workers at the end of 2012. However, discussions with local Chinese associations during an official visit by Premier Li Keqiang to Angola in May 2014 were predicated on a baseline 200,000 nationals in the country.[22] It is clear there are now several countries that – in terms of the number of Chinese citizens there – are 'too big to fail'. This means that the 'going-out' strategy orchestrated by the Ministry of Commerce and spearheaded by eager Chinese provinces now has to be squared with broader strategic calculations.

In our research and interviews with officials, we have encountered consistent under-reporting or lack of knowledge of the total number of Chinese abroad, such as during the evacuation from Libya at the start of the Arab Spring uprising against dictator Muammar Gadhafi. Similarly, while researching his book *China's Second Continent*, writer Howard French was told by the Chinese embassy that there were officially 5,000 Chinese in Mozambique, whereas the local Chinese community put the figure at 100,000.[23] Across Africa, the official number of Chinese workers at the end of 2012 stood at 200,000, compared to the more commonly repeated estimate of 2m, which itself could be an underestimate.[24]

Furthermore, a major difficulty in counting Chinese nationals overseas is that many are employed through specialised intermediaries, or 'foreign labour-service cooperation firms'. At the end of 2014, 892 such firms were registered with MOFCOM.[25] A company such as Beijing Construction Engineering Group Labour Service (BCEG) has 7,000 workers on international projects at any given time.[26] Part of this workforce is included in MOFCOM statistics, but a larger proportion deals directly with SOEs and operates without registering. One of MOFCOM's

Selected attacks on Chinese nationals 2004–15 (Refer to numbers on map ❶)

1. May 2004, Pakistan: 3 Chinese killed, 9 hurt, in Baluchistan car bombing near Gwadar port

2. Jun 2004, Afghanistan: 11 Chinese workers shot dead while asleep, 5 wounded, in attack on construction site south of Kunduz city

3. Oct 2004, Pakistan: 2 Chinese engineers taken hostage; 1 killed and 1 freed in Pakistani rescue operation in South Waziristan

4. Jan 2005, Iraq: 8 Chinese kidnapped by insurgents in Najaf. (Despite threats, all released unharmed)

5. Sep 2005, Thailand: 2 Chinese Muslim carpet sellers shot by insurgents in the restive southern province of Narathiwat

6. Feb 2006, Pakistan: 3 Chinese engineers shot dead by alleged terrorists in Baluchistan

7. Jan–Mar 2007, Nigeria: At least 16 Chinese oil, telecoms and other workers kidnapped in various incidents in southern Nigeria

8. Apr 2007, Ethiopia: 9 Chinese and 65 Ethiopians die in armed attack on Sinopec offices; another 7 Chinese workers kidnapped

9. May 2007, Somalia: One mainland Chinese crew member killed by pirates hijacking Taiwanese fishing vessel. (Rest of crew released Nov 2007)

10. Jul 2007, Pakistan: 3 Chinese workers shot dead, more wounded, in Peshawar reprisal for siege of Islamabad's Red Mosque. More than 100 died in the siege, after mosque-goers had kidnapped 'licentious' Chinese workers

11. Jun 2008, Thailand: Chinese carpet-seller killed in Narathiwat

12. Oct 2008, Sudan: Of 9 CNPC employees kidnapped in South Kordofan by rebels, 5 are killed in an attempted rescue

13. Aug 2009, Algeria: More than 10 Chinese business people injured during clashes with locals in Algiers

14. May 2010, Yemen: 2 Chinese oil workers kidnapped in Shabwa (released several days later)

15. Sep 2010, Sudan: 1 Chinese engineer killed and 1 wounded in armed attack on a South Kordofan oil field

16. Jan 2011, Sudan: 1 CNPC worker killed, 1 wounded, in South Kordofan gun attack

17. Feb 2011, Libya: Some 1,000 Chinese workers forced from their quarters during looting of Huafeng Construction site in Ajdabiya

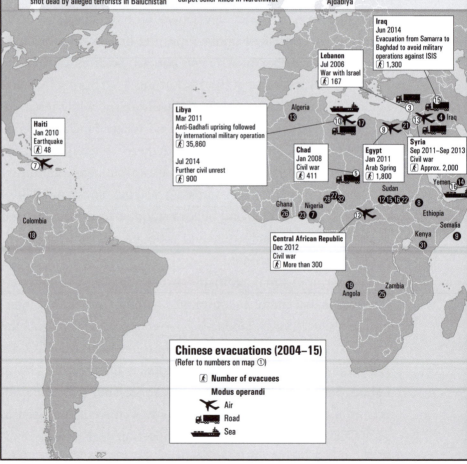

Iraq
Jun 2014
Evacuation from Samarra to Baghdad to avoid military operations against ISIS
👤 1,300

Lebanon
Jul 2006
War with Israel
👤 167

Libya
Mar 2011
Anti-Gadhafi uprising followed by international military operation
👤 35,860

Jul 2014
Further civil unrest
👤 900

Haiti
Jan 2010
Earthquake
👤 48

Chad
Jan 2008
Civil war
👤 411

Egypt
Jan 2011
Arab Spring
👤 1,800

Syria
Sep 2011–Sep 2013
Civil war
👤 Approx. 2,000

Central African Republic
Dec 2012
Civil war
👤 More than 300

Chinese evacuations (2004–15)
(Refer to numbers on map ①)

👤 **Number of evacuees**

Modus operandi

✈ Air

🚚 Road

🚢 Sea

18. Jun 2011, Colombia: 3 Emerald Energy workers kidnapped by FARC rebels in Caqueta province (released in Nov 2012)

19. Oct 2011, Angola: At least 5 Chinese workers have died in armed thefts in 2011, Xinhua reports

20. Oct 2011, Thailand: 13 Chinese sailors killed in attack on their cargo ships by suspected drug smugglers on the Mekong River

21. Jan 2012, Egypt: 25 Chinese workers at Egyptian state-owned cement factory kidnapped in Sinai by Bedouins (later freed)

22. Jan 2012, Sudan: 29 Sinohydro workers taken hostage by SPLM–N rebels (released after ICRC mediation)

23. Feb 2012, Nigeria: Captain of MV *Fourseas* SW Panamanian-flagged Chinese ship killed by pirates near Lagos port

24. Feb 2012, Pakistan: Pakistani Taliban militants claim responsibility for the killing of a Chinese woman in Peshawar, as revenge for the killing of Muslims in China's Xinjiang province

25. Aug 2012, Zambia: Chinese manager killed and another Chinese citizen injured by local coal miners during a pay protest

26. Oct 2012, Ghana: Chinese teenager shot dead and more than 100 Chinese nationals arrested during a crackdown on illegal gold miners in Ashanti region

27. Oct 2012, Nigeria: Chinese construction worker killed in Maiduguri, Borno state

28. Nov 2012, Nigeria: 4 Chinese killed in Borno state in 2 gun attacks; 2 police guards outside a worker's compound die in the first, 2 construction workers in the second

29. Jan 2013, Kyrgyzstan: At least 18 Chinese staff of Tebian Electric Apparatus hurt, 2 seriously, in dispute with locals after accusing villager of theft

30. Jun 2013, Pakistan: 3 Chinese climbers (and 8 others) die in a gun attack in Pakistan's mountainous north

31. Sep 2013, Kenya: 1 Chinese national killed, 1 injured in al-Shabaab attack on Westgate shopping mall, Nairobi

32. May 2014, Cameroon: Chinese workers leave Cameroon after 1 wounded, 10 go missing, in a suspected Boko Haram attack on Sinohydro facility in Waza, near Nigerian border

33. May 2014, Vietnam: 4 Metallurgical Corporation of China workers killed and hundreds of Chinese injured in anti-China riots across Vietnam over fishing rights

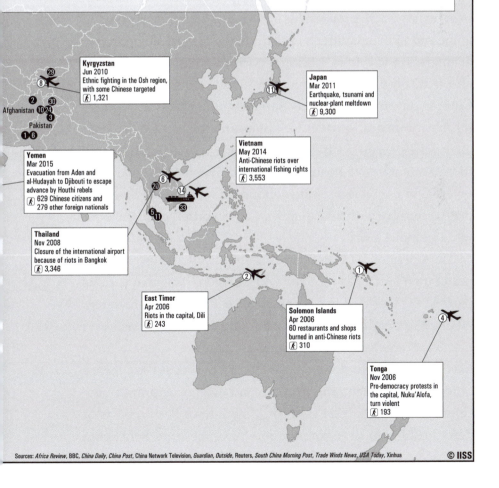

Kyrgyzstan
Jun 2010
Ethnic fighting in the Osh region, with some Chinese targeted
1,321

Japan
Mar 2011
Earthquake, tsunami and nuclear-plant meltdown
9,300

Afghanistan

Pakistan

Vietnam
May 2014
Anti-Chinese riots over international fishing rights
3,553

Yemen
Mar 2015
Evacuation from Aden and al-Hudayah to Djibouti to escape advance by Houthi rebels
629 Chinese citizens and 279 other foreign nationals

Thailand
Nov 2008
Closure of the international airport because of riots in Bangkok
3,346

East Timor
Apr 2006
Riots in the capital, Dili
243

Solomon Islands
Apr 2006
60 restaurants and shops burned in anti-Chinese riots
310

Tonga
Nov 2006
Pro-democracy protests in the capital, Nuku'Alofa, turn violent
193

Sources: *Africa Review*, BBC, *China Daily*, China Post, China Network Television, *Guardian, Outside*, Reuters, *South China Morning Post, Trade Winds News, USA Today*, Xinhua

© IISS

efforts to regulate labour overseas has been to enact regulations forcing these companies to register and share numbers with the government. This became a priority after the evacuation from Libya uncovered the enormous gap between official and real numbers (see Chapter Five).

Alongside workers employed directly or indirectly by major firms, many Chinese entrepreneurs have decided to pursue business opportunities overseas. In *China's Second Continent*, Howard French collected many personal stories of Chinese immigrants to African countries, many of them involved in small and medium-sized businesses, especially farming and services, without any backing from the state or any involvement in large SOE projects. He argues that labourers staying on at the end of their contracts constitute the biggest single source of migration to Africa.[27] Several African government officials and NGO representatives interviewed by French argue that the Chinese government actively supports emigration by requesting loose immigration rules for Chinese nationals. One Zambian interviewee accused China of 'offloading excess population'.[28] In our research, we heard similar complaints in Kazakhstan, where Chinese workers were denounced for supposedly entering the country with fake qualifications in order to obtain work visas and take jobs.[29]

The tendency of Chinese firms to employ their own nationals rather than locals has received widespread criticism in various parts of the world. It has become a threat in itself to the safety of Chinese employees in many countries, with backlashes in Zambia, Kyrgyzstan, Peru and other countries. Chinese firms have been accused of making predatory profits at the expense of local employment and growth, and even of a form of neo-colonialism.[30] In several countries, there have been reports of fierce hostility to large communities of Chinese workers living in closed compounds. Many senior SOE executives are aware of the risks inherent in this practice. In the words of the director of a large construction firm: 'You can't run away and build walls; the only solution is to mingle.'[31] Another problem with this practice is that it brings in lots of uneducated staff with zero awareness and knowledge of local culture and rules of behaviour. As a former executive with the oil major CNPC in Sudan argues: 'If you keep your eyes open and don't irritate the local population with insensitive behaviour, you reduce safety risks enormously.'[32]

The reality on the ground is nuanced, partly because the Chinese government and some firms are learning from mistakes, and partly as a direct consequence of the diversity of investment environments and corporate cultures. At one extreme, CITIC International Contracting brought 12,000 Chinese workers to fulfil a 2007 contract for construction of 20,000 housing units in a satellite Angolan city, and employed only 3,000 locals.[33] At the other extreme are construction projects carried out with a minimal number of Chinese staff, mostly engineers and foremen. The head of the Mombasa–Nairobi railway project, won in Kenya in August 2013 by China Road and Bridge Corporation, told the press that 2,000 Chinese employees and 30,000 Kenyans would carry out the work.[34] Some Chinese companies have adopted a localisation policy; CSCEC, for example, claims to have filled 61% of its project-management positions in Africa with local staff.[35]

The changing nature of the challenge

Attacks suffered by Chinese nationals overseas are under-reported by the media. There are examples of individuals killed without the knowledge of the local consular authorities because they were illegal immigrants or were otherwise not registered. Some attacks just do not attract attention because they are not political.

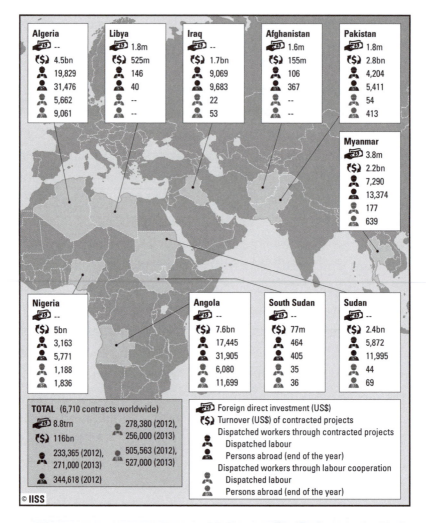

The map on pages 28–29, which compiles from open-source data the most significant attacks carried out against Chinese nationals, shows some 80 casualties between 2004 and 2014. The map shows a high concentration of attacks in Africa. Sudan, Nigeria and Pakistan stand out as the most dangerous countries for Chinese nationals in terms of casualties reported in the press. Although the politics of these countries differ, they all have in common a strong Chinese economic presence, a significant Chinese community, and a low level of public security with parts of their territory outside government authority.

Another way to appreciate the growing risks China faces abroad is to look at non-combatant evacuations, which have been relatively frequent in the past decade.

Chinese foreign policy is conducted in radically different conditions to those prevailing when the non-interference principle was adopted under Prime Minister Zhou Enlai in the 1950s. A veteran Chinese diplomat recalled that during his first posting in Kenya in the early 1980s, consular protection was not even part of the embassy's work – with good reason, for on the embassy's best estimates there were only five Chinese non-diplomats in the country.[36] The situation is only going to become more challenging in the coming years, with tourism, business travel, economic migration and 'labour cooperation' all expected to grow by double-digit figures.

Today, consular protection is already a priority task in many embassies, but protection and security have also become a priority for many others involved in Chinese operations overseas, including SOEs and government agencies.

The globalisation of Chinese economic and security interests is driving major change in China's foreign and security policies. Rather than being simply a developing country protecting its sovereignty, China has become a major power with national-security responsibilities stretching across the planet. And China's global risk map is constantly changing, as a result of corporate strategies and major foreign-policy decisions. Among those, Xi Jinping's 'New Silk Road', which proposes major infrastructure works along the ancient land and sea routes of the historic Silk Road, might have a major impact on the geography of risks and attacks in the next ten years.[37]

Notes

1 The 'going-out' strategy was first mentioned by Jiang Zemin in his report to the 16th Party Congress, 'Build a Well-off Society in an All-Round Way and Create a New Situation in Building Socialism with Chinese Characteristics', 8 November 2002, accessed at http://news.xinhuanet.com/english/2002-11/18/content_633685.htm.

2 'World Investment Report: Annex Tables', United Nations Conference on Trade and Development (UNCTAD), accessed at http://unctad.org/en/pages/DIAE/World%20Investment%20Report/Annex-Tables.aspx. The Ministry of Commerce (MOFCOM) puts the figures slightly higher, at US$107.8bn; see 'Joint Report on Statistics of China's Outbound FDI 2013 Released', MOFCOM, 12 September 2014, accessed at http://english.mofcom.gov.cn/article/newsrelease/significant news/201409/20140900727958.shtml.

3 'FDI in figures', OECD website, December 2014, accessed at http://www.oecd.org/daf/inv/FDI-in-Figures-Dec-2014.pdf.

4 'Brief Statistics on China Contracted Projects Overseas in 2013', MOFCOM, 17 January 2014.

5 Shuping Liao and Yongsheng Zhang, 'A new context for managing overseas direct investment by Chinese state-owned enterprises', East Asian Bureau of Economic Research Working Paper, no. 83.

6 Ibid.

7 'Emerging-market multinationals: The rise of state capitalism', The Economist, 21 January 2012.

8 Julie Jiang and Chen Ding, 'Update on Overseas Investments by China's National Oil Companies: Achievements and Challenges since 2011', International Energy Agency Partner Country Series, 2014.

9 Chinese scholar Zhu Feng quoted in Richard McGregor, 'Chinese diplomacy "hijacked" by big companies', Financial Times, 16 March 2008. See also David Shambaugh, China goes global: The partial power (Oxford: Oxford University Press, 2013), p. 169.

10 'China iron ore imports are set to rise', Wall Street Journal, 25 February 2014.

11 See, 'The 2013 Top 60 Chinese Contractors', Engineering News Record, accessed at http://enr.construction.com/engineering/pdf/top_lists/Top-Chinese-Contractors/2013-Top-60-Chinese-Contractors.pdf.

12 See 'Overseas Operations', CSCEC, accessed at http://english.cscec.com/art/2014/1/22/art_3536_125553.html.

13 'Zhongtie ji haiwai shouru zhan 1/3' (CREC aims at one-third of profits coming from overseas activities), Takungbao, 9 April 2014, accessed at http://news.takungpao.com/paper/q/2014/0409/2408192.html.

14 Henry Sanderson and Michael Forsythe, China's Superbank: Debt, Oil and Influence – How China Development Bank is Rewriting the Rules of Finance (Hoboken, NJ: John Wiley and Sons, 2013).

15 Barry Sergeant, 'China's $9bn "Deal of the century" with the DRC – A critical review', Mineweb, 10 March

2011. The value of the deal has since been revised and elements of it deferred; see Greg Ryan, 'Natural resource extraction in the DRC: China – saviour or plunderer?', *Consultancy Africa Intelligence*, 27 October 2013.

16 Senior academic, Author interview, Beijing, September 2014.

17 'Ling shiren zhumu de Zhongguo duiwai touzi yu jingji hezuo' (China's international economic cooperation and FDIs stuns the world), CHINCA, 22 September 2009, accessed at http://www.chinca.org:8080/cms/html/main/col145/2012-05/30/20120530021806171442066_1.html.

18 'Neidi jumin quannian chujing jin yi renci' (Number of nationals travelling abroad is approaching 100 million), *Fazhi Ribao*, 25 May 2014, accessed at http://www.chinanews.com/fz/2014/05-23/6203098.shtml.

19 'Waijiaobu guanyuan, 1 ming lingshiguan fuwu chao 19 wan haiwai zhongguo gongmin' (Diplomat: One consular officer for 190,000 Chinese nationals overseas), *Nanfang Dushibao*, 19 May 2014, accessed at http://news.sina.com.cn/c/2014-05-19/062030165037.shtml.

20 'Shangwubu guanyu jiaqiang duiwai touzi hezuo zaiwai renyuan fenlei guanli gongzuo de tongzhi' (MOFCOM's decision to improve the work related to the categorisation of personnel involved in investment cooperation overseas), MOFCOM, 4 November 2013, accessed at http://fec.mofcom.gov.cn/article/zcfg/zcfb/dwtz/201311/1782427_1.html.

21 '2013 nian woguo duiwai laowu hezuo yewu jianming tongji' (2013, China's labour-service cooperation with foreign businesses and concise statistics), MOFCOM, accessed at http://www.mofcom.gov.cn/article/tongjiziliao/dgzz/201401/20140100463572.shtml.

22 'Li Keqiang zai Angela zhaokai haiwai minsheng zuotanhui' (In Angola, Li Keqiang shares a roundtable discussion on the well-being of nationals overseas), Xinhua, 9 May 2014, accessed at http://www.xinhuaafrica.com/index.php?m=content&c=index&a=show&catid=15&id=5320.

23 Howard W. French, *China's Second Continent: How a Million Migrants are Building a New Empire in Africa*, (New York: Alfred A. Knopf, 2014).

24 *Ibid.*; Jacob Kushner, 'As Africa welcomes more Chinese migrants, a new wariness sets in', *Christian Science Monitor*, 4 September 2013; and Michelle Zhang, 'China's Views and Responses to Risk in Africa', *Africa Monitor* (Frontier Service Group), 3 October 2014.

25 'Field services company list', MOFCOM, accessed at http://wszw.hzs.mofcom.gov.cn/fecp/zsmb/corp/corp_ml_list1.jsp?ly=wplw.

26 Company profile, International Business Beijing Construction Engineering Group (BCEG), accessed at http://www.bceg.com.cn/about/ehsz_58.html.

27 French, *China's Second Continent*, p. 72.

28 *Ibid.*, p. 67.

29 Senior academic, Author interview, Astana, October 2012.

30 See, e.g., Lucy Ash, 'China in Africa: Developing ties', BBC News, 4 December 2007; and Xan Rice, 'China's economic invasion of Africa', *Guardian*, 6 February 2011.

[31] Director of SOE in construction sector, Author interview, Beijing, September 2014.

[32] *Ibid.*

[33] 'Zhongxin Guohua, Jiji lvxing qiye shehui zeren, shuli Zhongguo qiye lianghao xingxiang' (CITIC Guohua: Positively implement corporate social responsibility, establish a good image for Chinese firms), China International Contractors Association, accessed at http://www.chinca.org:8080/cms/html/shzr/col250/2012-05/30/201205300507 55328989819_1.html. However, the East–West Highway project in Algeria, a contract of approximately US$6.25bn won in May 2006 by a joint venture between CITIC and China Railway Construction Corporation, provides job opportunities for 13,000 Chinese, and 10,000 locals, according to CITIC. See 'Algeria East–West Expressway', 29 August 2008, accessed at http://big5.citic.com/trc/www.icc.citic.com/iwcm/null/null/ns:LHQ6LGY6LGM6MmM5NDgyOTUxYz BkMzY1YT AxMWMWwZGY1MTQwYz AwMDQscDosYTosbTo=/show.vsml.

[34] 'Liangqian zhongguoren kenniya xiu tielu, meimei fansi benguo hushi feizhou' (Two thousand Chinese repair railroad in Kenya, American media reflects how the US ignores Africa), *Huanqiu Shibao*, 8 August 2014, accessed at http://world.huanqiu.com/exclusive/2014-08/5099326.html.

[35] China State Construction Engineering Corporation Limited, accessed at http://english.cri.cn/7146/2010/10/14/2041s599398.htm.

[36] Retired Chinese ambassador, Author interview, Beijing, September 2014.

[37] 'China to establish $40 billion Silk Road infrastructure fund', Reuters, 8 November 2014. For details on the New Silk Road, see 'China's Initiatives on Building Silk Road Economic Belt and 21st-Century Maritime Silk Road', Xinhua, accessed at http://www.xinhuanet.com/english/special/silkroad/.

CHAPTER TWO

Transforming Chinese foreign policy and institutions

Within a decade, the protection of nationals abroad has steadily climbed the list of China's foreign and security priorities. In 2012, it was enshrined as a concept at the 18th Party Congress.[1] On a trip to Africa in May 2014, Chinese Premier Li Keqiang reiterated that it was a 'priority matter for the state' (*guojia toudeng dashi*).[2]

The year 2004 was an important turning point. In a few bloody months, 16 Chinese were killed in attacks in Sudan, Afghanistan and Pakistan, where Chinese state-owned companies were engaged on projects. The issue caught the attention of the top leadership in Beijing, but at the time both the government and companies venturing abroad only had limited experience in protecting nationals outside China.

Since then, the authorities have had to adapt to the rapid increase in numbers of Chinese travelling and working overseas, while at the same time facing greater public scrutiny of its foreign policy, especially with regards to the safety and rights of nationals abroad. The most outspoken voices on this subject tend to be nationalistic and always swift to criticise government inaction. It was as a result of these combined forces that China's top leadership found itself committing to protect Chinese nationals overseas.

Although the 'responsibility' to protect Chinese citizens abroad was not the direct result of grand strategy, it nonetheless helps to build the image of China as a great power. That, however, requires it to behave like other great powers and learn from their policies and experiences. For example, once it decided to evacuate Chinese workers from Libya in 2011, one of China's first moves was to ask the British Embassy in Beijing to share best practice for non-combatant evacuation operations.[3] The issue was also raised with the United States, France and Israel, three countries that sometimes resort to military means in evacuations and hostage-rescue situations.

The promise of protection to citizens overseas is part of a significant evolution of Chinese foreign policy in the past five years, one still taking shape under the leadership of President Xi Jinping. In 2010, analysts began using the term 'assertive' in describing a change in China's attitude towards its regional environment, especially its handling of territorial disputes with Japan, Vietnam and the Philippines.[4] At the same time, a major debate was unfolding among Chinese academics as to the continued relevance of former leader Deng Xiaoping's key foreign-policy guideline to 'bide time and build capacities' (*taoguang yanghui*).[5] The notion stressed the benefits of keeping a low profile, refusing to take the lead and maintaining a defensive and passive posture with regards to international security – all while accumulating relative power.

Although a conclusion to this academic debate was never spelled out publicly, the result appears clear several years into the Xi presidency: foreign policy is conducted in a less restrained way. Indeed, it was during the leadership handover from President Hu Jintao to Xi at the end of the 18th Party Congress in late 2012 that the policy was formally articulated.

A few months later, the 2013 Defence White Paper declared the protection of overseas energy resources and nationals abroad a major security concern to which the People's Liberation Army (PLA) might one day have to respond.

Responding to public scrutiny

Some of the roots of the shift lie in President Hu's new guidelines for diplomatic work in 2004, which raised for the first time the concept of 'diplomacy for the people' (*waijiao weimin*), the diplomatic interpretation of a 2003 slogan describing the Communist Party's new approach to governing: 'put the individual first' (*yiren weiben*).[6]

In response, the Ministry of Foreign Affairs (MFA) took steps to improve its consular protection work. The Ministry of Commerce (MOFCOM) spearheaded efforts to improve the regulatory framework governing the overseas activities of Chinese firms so that they were required to incorporate considerations of risks. The Ministry of Public Security (MPS) emerged as a new foreign-policy actor both on China's periphery and in Africa through cooperation with local law-enforcement agencies. At the same time, state-owned enterprises (SOEs) investing abroad, especially those with a record of being violently targeted, started elaborating their own security procedures. The State-owned Assets Supervision and Administration Commission of the State Council (SASAC), which oversees the largest SOEs, was also involved in shaping China's policy, as were the PLA, the National Development and Reform Commission (NDRC), and agencies involved in approving investments abroad.

The 2004 murders in Sudan, Afghanistan and Pakistan were widely covered in the Chinese media and sent shockwaves throughout the country. The Xinhua news agency set up a web page collating articles on the June 2004 killing in Afghanistan of 11 workers from the China Railway 14th Construction Bureau Group (Chapter Three). This Xinhua web page still includes links to more than 100 press articles, which question the responsibility for the attacks and the long-term impact of Afghan terrorism on Chinese security.[7]

Intense media coverage, internet users' below-the-line comments on articles, and discussions on social media have all been an integral part of the evolving domestic environment in which Chinese foreign policy is conducted. Most Chinese foreign-policy experts agree that the country's diplomacy is responsive to public expectations and that leaders do not wish to appear weak in the face of public demands for action. With nationalistic public opinion encountering little, if any, censorship, the protection of Chinese nationals overseas has become a hot-button issue regarding the dignity of the nation and the international capacity of the state. Many academics argue that China is selective when it comes to listening to public opinion on diplomatic matters, ignoring moderate voices while letting nationalist ones grow in influence.[8] Certainly, there are fewer and fewer moderate voices in the Chinese public debate on international relations.

Examples abound of acerbic criticism of inefficient consular assistance. The MFA has been a frequent target of online cynicism. It has also received calcium tablets in the post in a campaign to 'help' it 'strengthen its backbone' and deal forcefully with foreign countries.[9] Before the Libyan evacuation, an anxious post by a trapped Chinese expatriate on Sina Weibo, the largest social-media platform in China, caused netizens to respond by phoning the MFA in protest. Wrote one Weibo user: 'I just called the number 86-10-6596114 listed on the website of Ministry of Foreign affairs and a woman answered, sounding as if she's just woken up. As soon as the word "Libya" left my mouth, she said "the leaders have all gone home, we'll deal with it tomorrow".'[10]

Netizens swiftly advocate military intervention during crises, especially the use of special forces. After the kidnapping of 29 Sinohydro workers in Sudan in January 2012, a Weibo post read: 'If it was the United States or Russia, they would have air dropped in special commandos by now.'[11] After the kidnapping of four Chinese employees in Sudan in January 2013, harsh comments on Weibo urged 'send troops to Sudan' and 'pray for our fellow countrymen!'. Others suggested 'the moment when the government's ability will be tested has arrived'. 'Chinese people's passports have a statement that instructs them to not stir up trouble while abroad,' wrote one user. 'Americans' passports, on the other hand, say that America will always be behind you. This is one of the reasons why Chinese people are always bullied when they are abroad.'[12]

Such public pressure has sometimes pushed Chinese diplomacy to extra lengths. After the 2011 Christchurch earthquake in New Zealand – which took the lives of 23 Chinese students and others – embassy officials in Wellington requested extra compensation, for 'consolation' because of China's one-child policy and as a demonstration of the importance 'the New Zealand government attaches to Chinese international students'.[13]

Capacity-building in the State Council

Since President Hu's new guidelines for diplomatic work in 2004, three main Chinese government agencies have taken specific measures to build greater capacity and institutionalise their ability to extend greater protection to Chinese nationals abroad.

Ministry of Foreign Affairs

The MFA began institutionalising 'consular protection work' (*lingshi baohu gongzuo*) in 2004 under a newly established

Department for External Security Affairs. In November 2005, consular protection subsections of regional administrations in the Department of Consular Affairs were merged into a consular protection section. The new entity was staffed by seven diplomats in Beijing and handled 500 major matters during its first year of existence.[14] In August 2007, its consular work was further advanced with the creation of a Centre for Consular Protection. In 2013, it handled 31,000 consular events, or approximately 84 per day.[15]

The priority for China's consular services overseas is accessing information about Chinese nationals in their country of residence. As it is for other nations, it is a tremendous challenge for China to persuade its citizens to register with their local consulate. The massive scale of recent expatriation makes this challenge particularly daunting in the Chinese case. Interviews with officials and experts in Beijing suggest that the MFA is making little progress in this area. As a senior Chinese diplomat with long experience in Africa explained, 'It would be too costly for any embassy overseas to proactively obtain the numbers of Chinese nationals in African countries. We get some numbers from SOEs but individuals have no incentive to register. On top of that, the turnover is so fast that we can't remain constantly updated.'[16] Some Chinese experts see this as so problematic that they advocate making consular registration mandatory.[17]

These difficulties reflect the MFA's relatively low bureaucratic standing and its lack of capacity to direct SOEs, whose CEOs hold titles similar to government ministers and sometimes rank even higher in the party hierarchy.

Given this, the MFA has focused on improving communication with Chinese overseas. One tactic has been to automatically send the local embassy's contact details by text message to all subscribers of China Telecom and Unicom, the largest mobile-phone operators, once they switch on their telephone in a foreign country.[18] Another has been to create a central website with recommendations from consular services abroad regarding specific risks and the security environment in third countries.[19] However, according to Chinese diplomats, these advisories are mild and purposefully vague, because of China's fear of diplomatic complications; one example is the situation in Pakistan, which is perceived as extremely dangerous but presented with only a recommendation to 'refrain from unnecessary travel' inside the country.[20] A Chinese diplomat recalls that the construction of the website was very controversial, with many opposed to using language that could cause diplomatic offence.[21]

In 2013, the MFA at last introduced a new web page for electronic consular registration.[22] In early September 2014, Foreign Minister Wang Yi inaugurated the '12308', 24-hour consular-service hotline, and called upon staff to 'treat people in need of help as their own relatives, and to have the highest sense of responsibility'.[23] There are signs that these efforts will intensify in the near future. Experts already advocate making consular information available for the new tech-savvy generation on social-networking apps, such as QQ and We Chat.[24]

The MFA and embassies also play a leading role in the case of kidnappings. According to a senior Chinese diplomat, 'There is no complete ban on ransoms, we judge on a case-by-case basis. We see ransoms as last resort. We do not want to encourage rebels.' Instead, he says, China proposes 'development and infrastructure packages' in bargaining for hostages' release, 'but it does not work in all cases'.[25] Our research suggests that enterprises are more likely to pay a ransom than government agencies. The MFA has resorted to the mediation of the International Committee of the Red Cross (ICRC) in several cases, including in Sudan (see Chapter Six) and in Colombia.[26]

Diplomats also take the lead when safeguarding nationals overseas only involves consular protection. In Ghana, for example, the MFA, MPS and MOFCOM have established a joint working team led by the MFA director of the Centre for Consular Protection. In a mission to Ghana, they raised the issue of 'the Ghanaian government's action against illegal gold mining and the protection of legitimate rights and interests of the Chinese citizens in the country'.[27] The goal of the mission was to stop harassment of Chinese citizens involved in gold mining, some of them lured to Ghana by fake contracts. The team also met with illegal miners and urged them to shift to legal activities or return to China. Before the joint working team arrived in Ghana in June 2013, Accra had launched a crackdown on illegal mining. Some 1,072 Chinese – all from the same county in Guangxi Zhuang Autonomous Region – flew back to the homeland as a result of the crackdown.[28]

Despite these evolutions, MFA officials regularly complain publicly about the scarcity of the resources at their disposal. In 2014, the ministry says, each Chinese consular official provided services to 190,000 nationals overseas.[29] The number appears to aggregate the total of overseas travellers with other estimates, but the MFA has not explained how it reached that total. The Ministry of Human Resources and Social Security has power over the bureaucracy of the State Council, and the MFA does not have priority. Many other ministries complain that the MFA already enjoys favourable treatment, with comparably higher salaries for overseas postings and faster career mobility.[30] In the absence of further recruitment, the workload of the 600 or so diplomats in the Centre for Consular Protection will continue to increase in the foreseeable future.

Overall, having to protect nationals overseas has weakened the MFA. In November 2004, the State Council established a 'coordination committee for the protection of nationals and entities overseas' bringing 26 government agencies under MFA leadership.[31] But that MFA 'leadership' has been limited to convening meetings. The committee never evolved into one of the leaders of policy coordination within the Chinese system. Instead, the increasing power of the MPS (see below) has challenged the MFA's leadership in international negotiations related to nationals overseas. To ensure a smooth chain of command during a large evacuation, such as in Libya, requires leadership at a higher Communist Party level than is found within the MFA. The PLA, for example, is under direct Communist Party, rather than government, command.

Ministry of Commerce

MOFCOM is one of the most powerful ministries of the State Council. In charge of trade and international economic cooperation, its interest lies in the expansion and sustainability of Chinese business activities overseas. MOFCOM's responsibilities with regards to the security of Chinese nationals are not specified in the scope of its official mission. But as the agency in charge of drafting the regulatory environment in which Chinese firms operate abroad, it has inevitably emerged as a key actor in protecting Chinese citizens overseas.

Among the many provisions and regulations released by MOFCOM in the past decade, three stand out. The first was adopted in 2005 by the State Council at MOFCOM's initiative, with support from the MFA and SASAC. It is a communication sent to all provincial and local governments, and all entities under the State Council (including SOEs), entitled 'Views on Improving the Protection of Nationals and Entities Overseas'.[32] The text reflects MOFCOM's growing awareness of overseas security threats since the 2004 attacks. It calls on companies to improve security education for workers and to enhance their threat-assessment capabilities. It also advises firms to develop strict internal regulations to prevent incidents with the local population. Importantly, it calls on firms to make good use of the diplomatic resources of the nearest Chinese embassy or consulate. Most of the ideas now guiding the action of Chinese government agencies and firms were set out in this 2005 document.

Secondly, in 2010, MOFCOM issued 'Provisions on the Safety Management of Overseas Chinese-funded Enterprises and Personnel'.[33] The MFA, MPS, NDRC and SASAC also signed the text, a follow-up to the 2005 document designed to deal with an 'external security environment that has worsened' for Chinese firms and workers. The provisions aim to provide 'regulatory support to the smooth development of the going out strategy' (Article 1). Unlike the non-binding 2005 document, the 2010 provisions are mandatory measures that firms are obliged to abide by, although no penalties are specified.

The main merit of the document is that it addresses the security responsibilities of various actors and suggests a division of labour. It establishes the principle of a firm's responsibility for the security of its personnel under the notion that 'who sends personnel abroad is responsible for their safety' (*shei pai chu, shei fuze*). It holds companies responsible for providing sufficient security training to employees before dispatching them overseas, which includes educating them in the 'local customs and beliefs of the host country', while government agencies supervise these efforts. Overseas Chinese associations and chambers of commerce have a duty to 'provide support and guidance' on security matters. Embassies and diplomats are responsible for conducting regular assessments of the local security environment and providing 'guidance and supervision' to Chinese firms. The 2010 provisions also create the notion of a 'high-risk country'. They call on MOFCOM and the NDRC to review investment applications in such countries particularly thoroughly and to obtain the most updated security information from the local Chinese embassy.

The Libyan evacuation increased the government's awareness of the risks associated with investment and labour abroad, and MOFCOM brought provisions to a third level in 2012 by issuing the 'Regulations for the Management of Labour Service Cooperation'.[34] Under the regulations, foreign labour-service enterprises are now legally obliged to make a 'risk deposit' in a Chinese bank of at least 3 million RMB (US$482,000), for compensation and 'expenses required due to the occurrence of an emergency, repatriation of service personnel or acceptance of first-aid service'.[35]

Another important part of MOFCOM's role in security abroad is through approving overseas investments. MOFCOM shares this responsibility with the NDRC, and with SASAC when SOEs are involved. Under relaxed rules adopted in late 2013, the approval is only required for projects larger than US$1 billion or which involve 'sensitive countries and regions' or sensitive industries.[36] This is the latest development in a larger trend of gradually including security concerns in the approval procedure.

Finally, MOFCOM is involved in the field through its network of commercial attachés in Chinese embassies. In July 2014, some three years after the mass evacuation of Chinese nationals from Libya, these attachés took the lead in communicating with firms as 900 Chinese workers were evacuated from the North African country. An article in the Chinese press noted that while no information on the deteriorating security situation was communicated to Chinese companies before the February 2011 evacuation, the commercial section of the embassy had learned its lesson by 2014 and was able to communicate swiftly.[37]

Ministry of Public Security

In charge of law enforcement and domestic intelligence, the MPS traditionally operates on Chinese soil. Concerns about domestic stability in the past decade have led to enormous budget increases and increased prominence for the ministry. In 2013, China announced a domestic security budget of US$130bn, more than its military budget of US$102.4bn.[38] However, the elevation of the MPS in part came from the patronage of a powerful man who has now fallen from grace. As Minister for Public Security between 2002 and 2007, Zhou Yongkang spurred the minstry's rise. Between 2007 and 2012, he continued to have power over it, as a member of the Politburo Standing Committee (PSC) and head of the Communist Party's Central and Legislative Committee (the party structure over-seeing law enforcement and justice). However, three years after retiring at the 18th Party Congress, Zhou was charged with taking bribes, abuse of power and leaking state secrets in a case overturning PSC members' immunity.[39] Zhou's disgrace, and the fact that the MPS has not been represented in the PSC since the 18th Party Congress, puts in question the ministry's continued rise.

Nevertheless, in the years he spent at the apex of Chinese power, Zhou expanded the reach of China's MPS beyond the country's borders. In all likelihood, he was more sensitive to these issues because of his previous career in the oil industry. As general manager of China National Petroleum Corporation (CNPC) between 1996 and 1998, he advocated that CNPC should expand overseas exploration and development. He put this concept into practice in Sudan. Under his leadership, CNPC benefited from a framework agreement between Beijing and Khartoum and from an Exim Bank loan to start business in Sudan.[40] The protection of this investment would later entail complicated foreign-policy choices (see Chapter Six).

Under Zhou's leadership, the MPS developed its own foreign-policy agenda. The priority in terms of law enforcement overseas was to deny safe havens to Tibetan and Uighur pro-independence forces – an international extension of China's domestic security agenda that in certain nearby countries intersects with the protection of nationals overseas. For example, on his trip to Afghanistan in 2012, when Zhou was the highest-ranking Chinese official to visit since 1966, the protection of Chinese interests and citizens ranked high on his agenda (see Chapter Three).[41]

However, the MPS's overseas involvement grew mainly through the development of a network of MPS attachés in Chinese embassies and through cooperation with local law-enforcement agencies. Since 2006, when China had no extradition treaties, 37 have been concluded and 100 'justice assistance protocols' signed with other countries.[42] The aim was to be able to extradite those wanted for crimes in China.

There is nothing specific to China in the development of police diplomacy. Western countries also have domestic law-enforcement agencies represented in embassies, but mostly to handle illegal immigration and various forms of trafficking. A particularity of the Chinese approach is that it will investigate crimes committed abroad by Chinese nationals against their compatriots, via MPS agents operating on the ground. For example, in 2010 an investigation team with police officers from Sichuan, Guangxi and Fujian provinces successfully ended a prostitution ring sending southern Chinese women to the Democratic Republic of the Congo, with suspects detained in Kinshasa.[43] In 2012, the MPS repatriated a gang of 37 Chinese criminals targeting wealthy Chinese in Angola.[44]

The formal MPS presence overseas is small but significant. The ministry started posting representatives overseas in 1998.[45] In 2008, it had 30 police officers in 19 countries; by the end of

2012, this had grown to 38 officers in 23 countries.[46] In 2014, the MPS was represented in 27 countries.[47] There are three types of countries with an MPS presence: countries (mostly in Europe) where there are crimes against Chinese tourists; countries (mostly on China's periphery) with Uighur or Tibetan communities; and countries (in east Asia, Europe and Africa) where Chinese nationals commit crimes against other Chinese. Altogether, these footholds help China send task forces abroad to investigate crimes when needed. According to the MPS, in 2012 overseas liaison offices assisted in 812 cases of cross-border crime and deported 102 suspects.[48]

In late 2011, the MPS took the lead in investigating the massacre of 13 Chinese sailors on the Mekong River (see Chapter Four). The investigation resulted in the extradition, prosecution and execution of a Burmese gang leader and the decision to dispatch river patrols on the Mekong. The MPS took over from the MFA by the time it came to negotiating joint river and other law-enforcement patrols with Thailand, Laos and Myanmar. It was also an MPS official who revealed that China was considering what would have been a momentous step in authorising a targeted drone strike against the chief suspect in the murders.

Chinese companies abroad

Through their willingness to embark on projects in fragile states, Chinese state-owned enterprises have pulled the risk-averse Chinese government into dangerous conflict zones and compelled Chinese foreign policy to find pragmatic solutions to problems it had not intended to face. At the same time, these companies have been encouraged by a national policy supporting international expansion, in particular through easy access to credit. As major economic actors with large international activities encouraged by the government, SOEs are on the front line of risk management abroad. The protection of nationals overseas illustrates these state corporations' rise as international players. Private Chinese companies, including private security companies, have had less impact on Chinese foreign policy.

State-Owned Enterprises

To some degree, the protection of nationals overseas demonstrates the 'corporatisation' of China's foreign policy.[49] In Sudan and South Sudan, for example, the interests of CNPC have become entangled with the Chinese national interest (see Chapter Six). When Metallurgical Corporation of China (MCC) entered Afghanistan, despite the risks, it obliged the central Chinese authorities to pay more attention to Afghan national security (see Chapter Three).

Most Chinese companies investing abroad are SOEs, and their leadership is nominated by the Organisation Department, the Communist Party's secretive human-resources division.[50] However, far from simply implementing foreign-policy goals, the international expansion of SOEs is driven by commercial interest. Many of these companies, from oil majors in Sudan and Angola to construction companies in Libya and mining companies in Afghanistan, have shown an appetite for taking greater risk for greater potential gain. Even though the Chinese government's inherent risk-aversion is gradually being worn down and it is accepting a responsibility to protect Chinese citizens, the underlying questions of liability, risk management and costs are still unresolved. Is it the responsibility of the individual state-owned company or is it the duty of the Chinese government to ultimately save the day and foot the bill?

Many companies, especially the largest, are developing their own policies to manage risks overseas as part of their international business strategies. The same institutionalisation and capacity-building occurring in Chinese government agencies is proceeding in large state-owned firms too, for example, through the creation of risk-analysis units and research institutes. Although most staff members focus on economic research, more attention is being paid to political and geopolitical factors. Often, Chinese companies subcontract security assessment, as research by the Stockholm International Peace Research Institute (SIPRI) has documented. SIPRI has also studied how the purchase of insurance policies has influenced risk assessment – especially through the role of public insurance company Sinosure – and how the SASAC, NDRC and MOFCOM are trying to educate companies by using the investment-approval procedure as leverage.[51] On the ground, especially in the Middle East, some companies have recruited retired PLA officers to their staff. Praised for their organisational and logistics skills, these officers frequently also have knowledge of crisis management.[52]

There are several instances of large SOEs performing their own evacuations. CNPC, for example, evacuated its workers from Sudan without government support (see Chapter Six). Norinco, a major conglomerate active in arms, oil and construction, left Libya before the government evacuation effort began.[53] There are other examples of major companies contracting foreign private security firms to protect their installations and staff, for example in Afghanistan and Iraq.

Most of all, SOEs have had a direct impact on China's foreign policy. Corporate decisions taken by MCC in Afghanistan, CNPC in Sudan and construction companies in Libya, for example, have pushed the limits of the Chinese hands-off approach in risky security situations.

This pattern is particularly evident in arms sales, which in China involve certain authorised SOEs. These companies have their own commercial agenda and many willing international buyers, often in very fragile states. When China had less global exposure, it was easier to avoid any bad publicity from controversial arms sales. That has now changed. In Sudan, Darfuri rebels from the Justice and Equality Movement (JEM) deliberately attacked Chinese interests after learning that China was supplying arms to the regime in Khartoum. In Libya, it was harder for the Chinese government to create cordial ties with the country's new rulers when it was discovered that Chinese arms exporters had entered into talks with the previous Gadhafi regime, even after the 2011 uprising began.

Questionable sales by individual arms companies have an impact on China's national image, which in war-torn countries can jeopardise Chinese citizens. The government's response in this area was a regulatory one, when it decided to reform the arms export-control system to prevent damage to China's reputation.[54]

Private security contractors

Without robust regulation and transparency – and neither is a Chinese strong point – China may find itself with a 'Chinese Blackwater' case on its hands. Fortunately, the conditions are not yet in place for this to happen. With the exception of a few maverick pioneers, the security sector in China has been essentially publicly owned and focused on the domestic market. There have been very restrictive controls on firearms and extreme caution regarding international expansion.[55]

As a result, foreign companies are the main private providers of security to global Chinese companies, especially when armed force is needed. Often these private security operators are factored into Chinese firms' security policies. In Iraq, for example, CNPC uses military escorts provided by the Iraqi government from the airport to its work sites, while relying on a private Italian security firm to guard those sites.[56]

Nonetheless, the founder of Blackwater, Erik Prince, has established a Hong Kong-based security group specialising in 'securing supply chains' in Africa. The executive directors of Prince's new Frontiers Service Group include former top executives at China International Trust and Investment Corporation (CITIC), a major globalised SOE. According to the Chinese press, CITIC owns 20% of Frontiers Service Group.[57] Prince has also recruited former MPS officials to senior leadership positions.[58] The group's Beijing office also has a research department that focuses on risk analysis for Chinese SOEs and government agencies.

Some in China have warned against embracing a Blackwater strategy (using non-Chinese private security contractors) and suggested that Beijing instead explore the internationalisation of its domestic security industry. The argument is that the Blackwater model fits 'US gun culture' and Washington's involvement in wars in Afghanistan and Iraq; without these the enterprise would not have gained such influence (before the scandal of killing Iraqi civilians precipitated its downfall).[59] As China has almost 4,000 security companies in the domestic market, it only needs state support to begin to globalise the industry.[60] Such support is still lacking, with the deputy foreign minister Zhang Zhijun on record in late 2012 stating clearly that private security companies had 'no power to enforce laws overseas' and no major sign of upcoming reforms of the regulatory environment or the national policy.[61] Today, the use of firearms by private Chinese security contractors abroad remains a hypothetical problem.

Force as the ultimate foreign-policy option

In recent years, the involvement of the PLA in the protection of Chinese nationals overseas has grown substantially. Officially, the military remains a force in the background that only intervenes in a tiny minority of cases. However, its incremental participation raises some important questions about the future role of the military as a foreign-policy tool. At the highest strategic level, the protection of overseas nationals has been formally included in the PLA's missions since the 2013 Defence White Paper. The military has also embraced the American concept of 'Military Operations Other than War' since 2008.[62] But there are few indications as to which type of operations the PLA would consider to come under this. Is China training special forces to liberate hostages? Is the PLA prepared to establish a safety perimeter in a foreign land to facilitate a secure evacuation? Are overseas bases among the tools for protecting nationals abroad? Could targeted assassinations be used in response to the murder of Chinese nationals?

These remain open questions. However, lessons can be drawn from previous developments and PLA operations, including in multinational anti-piracy patrols in the Gulf of Aden, the evacuation from Libya and United Nations peace-keeping in Sudan. The nature of these three missions – escort, evacuation and peacekeeping operations – points to China's great caution in the use of military assets abroad. At the same time, these are three milestones in the use of Chinese military power abroad, and in a period of just five years, which all relate to the protection of nationals and assets overseas.

The 2009 decision to dispatch PLA Navy (PLAN) flotillas to the Gulf of Aden on a mission against Somali pirates, for instance, came in response to threats to the lives and livelihoods of Chinese sea traders. According to retired PLA colonel Yue Gang, around half a million Chinese are employed on ships in the maritime-transportation sector (accounting for 5% of the global industry).[63] Before UN Security Council resolutions paved the way for an international naval operation, the insurance costs of travelling through the region had become prohibitive for many Chinese shipping operators.[64] Therefore, in coordinating with the UN-sanctioned international security operation, China was also pursuing self-serving goals – such as force-projection training for the PLAN. For the PLAN, having a flotilla operating on a rotating basis far from Chinese coasts was a major step, while working with partners to combat piracy was a public-diplomacy coup. Before the decision was made, the Chinese government carefully collected feedback from other, particularly African, countries to ensure there would be no negative implications for China's image in the region. Once the flotillas were in place, the PLA released promotional materials, containing operational details, to highlight the Chinese contribution. This was in contrast to the relative silence surrounding other aspects of China's military modernisation.

A second turning point was the role of the PLA in the 2011 evacuation from Libya. The PLAN diverted the frigate *Xuzhou* from patrols in the Gulf of Aden to monitor the coast of Libya, to gain situational awareness and to deter any attacks on ferries evacuating Chinese nationals. The PLA Air Force's (PLAAF) mission was different. IL-76 military transport aircraft directly evacuated nationals from the desert of Libya, where only military planes could land safely on the poor-quality runway. The choice of Khartoum as the first stop on the evacuation route is interesting, as Khartoum was also a hub for Chinese civilian planes in the South Sudan evacuation in 2013. Its repeated use could be an early sign of China's developing so-called dual-use logistics facilities to allow flexible power projection abroad – instead of relying on basing agreements along American lines.[65] The PLAN played an even greater role in non-combatant evacuation operations in Yemen in March 2015. Rather than monitoring the situation and deterring attacks, two frigates deployed in the Gulf of Aden were diverted to Aden and al-Hudaydah to themselves evacuate 629 nationals. In a display of China's new overseas capabilities, the Chinese warships also carried 279 foreign nationals to safety.

A third notable development has been the recent decision by the PLA to take up combat roles in UN peacekeeping missions. In the past, Chinese blue helmets had non-combatant roles as administrative staff, engineers, transport and hospital workers, security guards, military observers and civilian police.[66] However, in late 2014 China decided to send a battalion of 700 combat troops to join the UN Mission in South Sudan (UNMISS) – a move portrayed in some Western media as an attempt to protect Chinese oil workers in the war-torn country.[67] Rather than direct intervention, it was about working within the UN system and empowering a peacekeeping mission to help protect Chinese interests, which in this case coincide with those of the international community.

Looking ahead, the PLA now has many assets that could be deployed in non-combatant evacuations, even in hostile territory. Among these are the Type-071 Landing Platform Docks (LPDs) being produced for the PLAN. The first LPDs to enter service, from 2007, gave the PLAN its first amphibious lift capability. Because of their capacity to accommodate large numbers of troops and armoured vehicles, they could also evacuate civilians. Their helicopter deck could be used for even more precise extraction missions, for example from an embassy compound or a particular factory. The PLAN has also commissioned a hospital ship, the *Peace Ark*, which would certainly be deployed if the military had to conduct an evacuation under extreme conditions. Were this the case, one can easily imagine a PLAN task force comprised of these two types of ships under the protection of one or two frigates or destroyers for, say, suppression of enemy fire from shore. In an extreme scenario, with the need for air cover to conduct an evacuation, the PLAN would need to deploy an aircraft carrier battle group.

Special-forces units might also be deployed in an evacuation mission. Although information is available on the organisation and capacities of Chinese special forces, little is known about their doctrine, and it remains unclear whether they train for hostage-rescue missions overseas. However, it is worth noting that special forces have sailed aboard all Chinese anti-piracy missions in the Gulf of Aden.[68]

The 2013 Defence White Paper's inclusion of the protection of nationals overseas only describes missions the PLA is already conducting. In recent years, no doctrine has been made public regarding future non-combatant evacuations, and there is no evidence that the PLAN and PLAAF are training for such missions.

However, the question of future non-combatant evacuations impinges on two major ongoing strategic debates. Firstly, should China develop a 'Mahanian navy', following the precepts of Alfred Thayer Mahan, the leading nineteenth-century American naval strategist who insisted that having a strong navy to protect trade routes was the key condition for being a great power? So far, China is developing power-projection capabilities, but the balance China should strike between its naval power and land forces remains an open question. Its strategists disagree over whether classical concepts of land and maritime power apply to China.[69]

Secondly, in a closely related question, the Chinese strategic community has debated for years the topic of overseas bases. So far, the PLAN is using 'places' rather than 'bases' in logistical support to its mission in the Gulf of Aden – regularly pulling into port in Aden, Djibouti, Salalah (in Oman), Karachi, Colombo and Singapore.[70] Media reports have often suggested that the PLA is in discussions about a permanent naval base in Pakistan, Sri Lanka or the Maldives, as part of a 'string of pearls' strategy to protect sea lanes of communication in the Indian Ocean.[71] Chinese officials have always denied such plans, and the PLAN's current arrangements are probably sufficient unless it significantly increases its operations in the Indian Ocean.[72]

New capacities to serve greater ambitions

The shifts in China's foreign policy to ensure greater protection of nationals overseas reflect the evolving relationship between public opinion, government legitimacy, China's evolving security interests and its gradual move towards great-power status.

With a strong commitment from Chinese leaders and under greater public scrutiny, many Chinese government agencies and the PLA are now paying close attention to the protection of nationals overseas. They have adjusted their operations, but with no clear overall plan other than a signal from the top of the Communist Party that the issue had to be prioritised. Consequently, they now have the capacity and, to some degree, standard operating procedures to prevent and manage crises overseas. Although no government agency is clearly leading this policy change, coordination between the numerous agencies involved is not a problem in practice. The only exception is when it comes to risk prevention and proactive risk management, which are still extremely fragmented activities and ultimately depend on corporate behaviour. Government agencies and the PLA have all tested new ways of coping with problems, and there is no reason to believe that they will not continue to innovate.

However, protecting nationals overseas is not only a technical matter requiring efficient consular protection, swift evacuations and sophisticated protection work. It has political and strategic implications. It raises questions about the impact of Chinese actions in third countries, and whether and how

Chinese foreign policy can have a positive impact on these countries' domestic security.

Ultimately, the responsibility to protect Chinese interests abroad entails a more pragmatic interpretation of the principle of non-interference – to the point of even relinquishing a hands-off approach in countries where Chinese interests are most threatened. This responsibility compels the Chinese government to engage with many other forces, such as rebel groups and militants, so as to hedge its bets in countries in transition, such as Afghanistan and Libya. In other words, the answer to the new risks China faces overseas lies in greater involvement, via once rarely used diplomatic tools, such as mediation, diversification of interlocutors and power projection. The term 'creative involvement', coined by Peking University scholar Wang Yizhou to describe Chinese foreign-policy innovation in recent years, suggests a middle way for involvement short of interference. To a certain extent, this describes the evolution of China's foreign policy to date.[73]

These changes within the Chinese political system raise the lingering possibility of China's use of force overseas. Even though some SOEs have contracted foreign firms to protect their installations and staff in the war zones of Afghanistan and Iraq, there remains resistance in China to the idea of a Chinese private security sector. So the question for the international security order really is the likelihood of Chinese military operations abroad if a crisis seriously jeopardises the security of Chinese nationals. China has always been reluctant to take such a step, and it has always had other options, including evacuation. However, its willpower not to intervene has never yet been tested head on.

Notes

1 Michael Swaine, 'The 18th Party Congress and Foreign Policy: The Dog that Did Not Bark?', *China Leadership Monitor*, vol. 40, Winter 2013.

2 'Li Keqiang feizhou tan zhong qiye zouchuqu, minsheng shi toudeng dashi' (Li Keqiang talks of Chinese firms going out in Africa, welfare is a priority matter), *Zhongguo Xinwen Wang*, 9 May 2014, accessed at http://finance.sina.com.cn/world/20140509/150719058167.shtml.

3 British military officer, Author interview, Beijing, January 2013.

4 The term was popularised by a series of articles published by Michael Swaine, including 'China's assertive behavior, part one, on core interests', *China Leadership Monitor*, 15 November 2010.

5 François Godement, 'Introduction, Geopolitics on Chinese Terms', *China Analysis*, European Council on Foreign Relations, October 2010.

6 'Put the individual first' is the core concept of Hu Jintao's 'scientific development theory' formally adopted at the Third Plenum of the 16th Central Committee in October 2003.

7 'Chinese workers attacked in Afghanistan', Xinhua, accessed at http://news.xinhuanet.com/world/2004-06/10/content_1518966.htm.

8 Zheng Wang, *Never Forget National Humiliation – historical memory in Chinese politics and foreign relations* (New York: Columbia University Press, 2012).

9 Numerous Chinese diplomats, Author interviews, 2011–13.

10 'China's other problem with protests abroad', *Wall Street Journal*, 23 February 2011.

11 'Kidnappings of Workers Put Pressure on China', *New York Times*, 31 January 2012.

12 'Kidnappings in Sudan prompt outrage on Chinese social networks', China–Africa Project, 16 January 2013.

13 'China wants extra compensation for Christchurch Quake Victims', *New Zealand Herald*, 14 March 2011.

14 MFA, *Zhongguo Lingshi Gongzhu* (*The Consular Affairs of China*) (Beijing: Shijie Zhishi Press, 2014), p. 335.

15 'Waijiaobu ruhe chuli Zhongguo ren haiwai bangjiao shijian' (Foreign Affairs: How to deal with the abduction of Chinese citizens abroad), *Takungbao*, 26 August 2014, accessed at http://news.takungpao.com/world/watch/2014-08/2694753.html.

16 Retired senior Chinese diplomat, Author interview, Beijing, 12 September 2014.

17 Li Xiaomin, 'Lingshi baohu jizhi reng you chuangxin yudi' (Still room to innovate in China's consular protection system), *Huanqiu Shibao*, 8 January 2014, accessed at http://opinion.huanqiu.com/opinion_world/2014-01/4732722.html.

18 Chinese diplomat, Author interview, Beijing, February 2012.

19 Consular service website of the MFA, accessed at http://cs.mfa.gov.cn/gyls/szzc/.

20 'Briefing on Pakistan', MFA, accessed at http://cs.mfa.gov.cn/zggmcg/ljmdd/yz_645708/bjst_645958/.

21 Chinese diplomat, Author interview, Beijing, September 2014.

22 Electronic consular registration service, MFA, accessed at http://ocnr.mfa.gov.cn/expa/.

23 'Haiwai Zhongguo gongmin yu jingji qingkuang ke da waijiaobu 12308 dianhua' (Overseas Chinese nationals encountering emergency situations can dial 12308 and reach the MFA), Xinhua, 2 September 2014, accessed at http://news.sina.com.cn/c/2014-09-02/164430783553.shtml.

24 Li Xiaomin, 'Lingshi baohu jizhi reng you chuangxin yudi' (Still room to innovate in China's consular protection system).

25 Retired senior Chinese diplomat, Author interview, Beijing, 12 September 2014.

26 'All 29 kidnapped Chinese workers in Sudan freed', Xinhua, 7 February 2012; and 'Four Chinese kidnap victims freed in Colombia', *Latin American Herald Tribune*, 22 November 2012.

27 MFA, 'Joint Working Team of the Ministries of Foreign Affairs, Commerce and Public Security Makes Representations to Ghana over Protection of Chinese Gold Miners' Safety and Legitimate Rights', 12 June 2013, accessed at http://au.china-embassy.org/eng/xw/t1050690.htm.

28 '1,072 Chinese Gold Miners Return from Ghana', *People's Daily*, 14 June 2013.

29 'Waijiaobu guanyuan, 1 ming lingshiguan fuwu chao 19 wan haiwai zhongguo gongmin' (Diplomat: One consular officer for 190,000 Chinese nationals overseas), *Nanfang Dushibao*, 19 May 2014, accessed at http://news.sina.com.cn/c/2014-05-19/062030165037.shtml.

30 MFA personnel, Author interview, Beijing, September 2014.

31 MFA, *Zhongguo Lingshi Gongzhu* (*The Consular Affairs of China*), p. 333.

32 'Guanyu jiaqiang jingwai zhongzi qiye jigou yu renyuan anquan gongzuo de yijian' (Regarding the improvement of the work to provide safety to Chinese firms and employees overseas), MOFCOM, MFA, SASAC, 28 September 2005, accessed at http://www.gov.cn/zwgk/2005-10/19/content_79807.htm.

33 'Jingwai zhonzi qiye jigou he renyuan anquan guanli guiding' (Regulations regarding safety management of Chinese firms and employees overseas), amended version, MOFCOM, 15 February 2012, accessed at http://www.mofcom.gov.cn/aarticle/i/jyjl/k/201202/20120207967105.html.

34 'Duiwai laowu hezuo guanli tiaoli' (Regulations on management of foreign labour service cooperation), MOFCOM, 13 June 2012, accessed at http://www.china.com.cn/policy/txt/2012-06/11/content_25617861.htm.

35 Mathieu Duchâtel, Oliver Bräuner and Zhou Hang, 'Protecting China's Overseas Interests, the Slow Shift Away from

Non-Interference', Stockholm International Peace Research Institute (SIPRI) Policy Paper No. 41, June 2014, pp. 49–50.

36 'MOFCOM announces new rules on Chinese overseas investment', *Global Times*, 8 September 2014.

37 'Zhongguo lingshi baohu jizhi jian chengshu' (The Chinese consular protection system is increasingly mature), *Liaowang*, 10 August 2014, accessed at http://www.lwgcw.com/NewsShow.aspx?newsId=36245.

38 'China withholds full domestic security spending figure', Reuters, 4 March 2014.

39 'China's ex-security chief Zhou Yongkang charged with corruption, leaking secrets', *South China Morning Post*, 4 April 2015.

40 Luke Patey, *The New Kings of Crude; China, India and the Global Struggle for Oil in Sudan and South Sudan* (London: C. Hurst & Co., 2014), pp. 89–97.

41 Raffaello Pantucci and Alexandros Petersen, 'Shifts in Beijing's Afghan Policy: A View from the Ground', *China Brief* (Jamestown Foundation), vol. 12, no. 21, 5 November 2012.

42 David Shambaugh, *China goes global: the partial power* (Oxford: Oxford University Press, 2013), p. 146.

43 'Gang busted for trafficking women in Congo', *South China Morning Post*, 4 December 2010.

44 'Chinese gangsters repatriated from Angola', *Telegraph*, 26 August 2012.

45 'Zhuwai jingwu lianluo guan, zou xiang shijie de Zhongguo jingcha mingpian' (Chinese liaison offices abroad: the international business card of Chinese police), *Renmin gong'an bao* (*Journal of Chinese police*), 14 January 2014, accessed at http://www.cpd.com.cn/n10216060/n10216144/c21167876/content.html.

46 'Gong'anbu xiang 19 ge guojia paizhu 30 ming jingwu lianluoguan' (The MPS has dispatched 30 liaison officers in 19 countries), Xinhua, 1 December 2008; and 'Woguo xiang 23 ge guojia paizhu jingwu lianluoguan' (China has MPS liaison offices in 23 countries), Xinhua, 25 December 2012.

47 These are: 1) Argentina; 2) Saudi Arabia; 3) Tajikistan; 4) Laos; 5) Kazakhstan; 6) Turkey; 7) Malaysia; 8) Vietnam; 9) Angola; 10) Mongolia; 11) Afghanistan; 12) Pakistan; 13) Philippines; 14) South Korea; 15) Japan; 16) Myanmar; 17) Thailand; 18) South Africa; 19) Germany; 20) Russia; 21) France; 22) Kyrgyzstan; 23) Uzbekistan; 24) Italy; 25) United States; 26) United Kingdom; and 27) Canada. See the MPS website at http://www.mps.gov.cn/.

48 'Zhuwai jingwu lianluo guan, zou xiang shijie de Zhongguo jingcha mingpian' (Chinese liaison offices abroad: the international business card of Chinese police).

49 Duchâtel, Bräuner and Zhou, 'Protecting China's Overseas Interests, the Slow Shift Away from Non-Interference'.

50 Erica S. Downs and Michal Meidan, 'Business and Politics in China, the Oil Executive Reshuffle of 2011', *China Security*, vol. 19 (2011), pp. 3–21.

51 Duchâtel, Bräuner and Zhou,, 'Protecting China's Overseas Interests, the Slow Shift Away from Non-Interference'.

52 Manager of a private Western security company, Author interview, Beijing, September 2014.

53 Norinco manager, Author interview, October 2012.

54 Mark Bromley, Mathieu Duchâtel, Paul Holtom, 'China's Exports of Small Arms and Light Weapons', SIPRI Policy Paper No. 38, October 2013.

55 Mathieu Duchâtel, Oliver Bräuner and Zhou Hang, 'Protecting China's Overseas Interests, the Slow Shift Away from Non-Interference', pp. 55–6.

56 'A day in the life of a Chinese worker in Iraq', Caixin, 15 July 2014.

57 'Meiyongbing zhiwang zhezhang Zhongguo gongsi jiang lingdao kaituo feizhou yewu' (The American king of war establishes a Chinese company to support business activities in Africa), Tengxun, 8 August 2014, accessed at http://news.qq.com/a/ 20140808/ 022083.htm.

58 Frontiers Service Group, accessed at http://www.fsgroup.com/team/.

59 In September 2007, Blackwater guards shot 17 Iraqi civilians dead and injured 20 in a square in Baghdad. The killings outraged locals. In 2014, one Blackwater employee was convicted of murder, and three of manslaughter; see Matt Apuzzo, 'Blackwater Guards Found Guilty in 2007 Iraq killings', New York Times, 22 October 2014.

60 Luo Ying, 'Blackwater poor example for Chinese security companies going global', Global Times, 12 August 2014.

61 Zhang Haizhou, 'Protection of overseas citizens and assets proposed', China Daily, 3 September 2012.

62 M. Taylor Fravel, 'Economic Growth, Regime Insecurity and Military Strategy: Explaining the Rise of Noncombat Operations in China', Asian Security, vol. 7, no. 3 (2011), pp. 177–200.

63 Yue Gang, 'Zhongguo junli ying hanwei haiway liyi, jue bu rongren paihua beiju zaiyan' (The Chinese military must protect overseas interests and never tolerate again an anti-China tragedy), Sina.com, 18 April 2013, accessed at http:// mil.news.sina.com.cn/2013-04-18/0824722110.html.

64 Chinese national-security expert, Author interview, Beijing, November 2011.

65 See a full catalogue of China's basing options in Christopher D. Yung and Ross Rustici with Scott Devary and Jenny Lin, 'Not an Idea We have to Shun': Chinese Overseas Basing Requirements in the 21st Century (Washington DC: National Defense University Press, 2014).

66 Bates Gill and Huang Ching-Hao, 'China's expanding role in peacekeeping', SIPRI Policy Paper No. 25, November 2009.

67 'China deploys troops in South Sudan to defend oil fields, workers', Wall Street Journal, 9 September 2014.

68 Dennis J. Blasko, 'Chinese Special Operation Forces: Not Like Back at Bragg', War on the Rocks, 1 January 2015.

69 Duchâtel, Bräuner and Zhou, 'Protecting China's Overseas Interests, the Slow Shift Away from Non-Interference', pp. 14–17.

70 Daniel Kostecka, 'Places and Bases: The Chinese Navy's Emerging Support Network in the Indian Ocean', *Naval War College Review*, vol. 64, no. 1 (Winter 2011), pp. 59–78.

71 Daniel Kostecka, 'Hambantota, Chittagong and the Maldives – Unlikely Pearls for the Chinese Navy', *China Brief* (Jamestown Foundation), vol. 10, no. 23, 19 November 2010.

72 'China denies reports to set up 18 naval bases in Indian Ocean', *Economic Times*, 27 November 2014.

73 Wang Yizhou, *Chuanzaoxing Jieru, Zhongguo waijiao de xin quxiang* (*Creative Involvement, a new direction for Chinese foreign policy*) (Beijing: Peking University Press, 2013).

CHAPTER THREE

China's 'AfPak' hinterland

Afghanistan and Pakistan provided China with some early lessons in the vulnerability of nationals overseas. Two attacks in quick succession in summer 2004 – one in May in Gwadar, Pakistan, that killed three, and another in June in Kunduz, Afghanistan, killing 11 – were a clear wake-up call to government agencies in Beijing. Chinese security analysts have long worried that terrorist groups in the two countries might turn their attention to Chinese interests, and the 2004 attacks seemed to confirm their worst fears.

In the years that followed, Afghanistan and Pakistan emerged as major concerns for China's national security, as violence in Pakistan grew and the situation in Afghanistan barely improved. In Afghanistan and in Pakistan's tribal areas, Uighur militants have often fought alongside Taliban and other terrorists. In Afghanistan, these groups have mainly targeted Western forces, and in Pakistan they have mainly attacked the government and other perceived enemies. However, the risk of Islamic terrorist activity in the restive, ethnic-Uighur-dominated Chinese province of Xinjiang has blurred the distinction between China's domestic security and the protection of nationals and assets in neighbouring Central Asia.[1]

Although China has only provided limited evidence that attacks in Xinjiang had organisational links to terrorist groups in Afghanistan and Pakistan, concerns have intensified that such links might develop – especially as terrorist attacks on Chinese soil have dramatically increased, including a shocking knife attack by Uighur fighters at Kunming train station in 2014.

Facing those risks, China had to adjust its policies. With the drawdown of Western forces from Afghanistan looming, China appeared in 2015 to be readying itself for deeper engagement in the region.

China's risky business ventures in Afghanistan

In sympathy with the United States after the attacks of 11 September 2001, China voted for all of the Security Council resolutions giving support to the NATO-led military intervention in Afghanistan to hunt down mastermind Osama bin Laden and remove the Taliban regime that had given him sanctuary. China neither sent combat troops to the country nor provided any support to the International Security Assistance Force. After the beginning of military operations in October 2001, however, China quickly affirmed a commitment to supporting the economic reconstruction of the country. This was reaffirmed to Afghan President Hamid Karzai during his visit to Beijing in January 2002.

In Chinese diplomatic language, economic development is intimately linked to security and stability. For example, speaking at the United Nations in 2011 about preventive diplomacy, then-Foreign Minister Yang Jiechi argued: 'Only by helping the countries concerned realize economic growth, social progress and sustainable development and eliminate the economic and social causes for conflicts, can we fundamentally prevent the conflicts from happening.'[2] This has always applied to Afghanistan, where most Chinese analysts see the country's economic underdevelopment as the root cause of the violence plaguing it.

Many in the West have accused China of 'free-riding' on the US and NATO military presence in Afghanistan to pursue economic and strategic interests without bearing the costs of security itself.[3] The Chinese response to this criticism has always been to highlight its projects' potential contribution to Afghan development. However, China's involvement in Afghanistan's economic development has not resulted in any improvement of the security situation. On the contrary, Chinese projects have fallen victim to the security situation in Afghanistan, despite Chinese companies' good intentions and willingness to take great risks.

Economic development was certainly the initial spin put on the new copper mine at Mes Aynak, 40 kilometres from Kabul in Logar province, where in 2007 Metallurgical Corporation of China (MCC) and Jiangxi Copper Corporation (JCC), a central and provincial SOE respectively, won a competitive tender for a 30-year lease. The US$3.4 billion contract represented the largest investment in the history of Afghanistan.[4] The scale of Aynak – estimated to contain the world's second-largest copper deposits, worth some US$100bn – could generate considerable tax revenues for the Afghan central government, in the form of a generous 20% royalty and a bonus payment of US$808 million.[5] China's investment in the project was also to play a significant role in infrastructure development, as Beijing agreed to build a power plant, a water supply and purification system, a coal mine, a smelter to refine copper ore and a railway to Pakistan.[6] The World Bank estimated that Aynak could create '4,500 direct, 7,600 indirect and 62,500 induced jobs' as a result of the economic development it would bring to the country.[7]

If security concerns were downplayed during contract negotiations, MCC and JCC soon had to face the reality on the ground. After a high-profile rocket attack by Taliban militants in August 2012, news surfaced of 19 earlier attacks on the mine[8] and of repeated threats to abduct staff[9] as insurgents sought to interrupt one of Kabul's highest-profile projects. Although there were fewer than 200 Chinese workers at Mes Aynak at the time of the August 2012 attack, most of them were afterwards sent home for an unspecified period.[10] Many apparently returned, but in June 2013 MCC workers were reportedly threatening to quit if their safety was not guaranteed.[11]

Reports soon began to emerge that MCC wished to renegotiate the terms of the mining contract with the Afghan authorities, forsaking its commitments to building infrastructure and cutting its royalties and the bonus payment.[12] The discovery of a 1,400-year-old Buddhist monastery on the site has thrown the mine into further doubt,[13] despite a discussion about reviving the project between new Afghan President Ashraf Ghani and his Chinese counterpart Xi Jinping during a summit in Beijing in October 2014.[14] In late 2014, MCC was apparently trying to negotiate a postponement until 2019, while Afghan authorities struggled to convince the Chinese company that on-site security was guaranteed.[15]

At another flagship project, China's largest state-owned oil firm, China National Petroleum Corporation (CNPC), faced similar difficulties. In a joint venture with Afghan partner Watan Oil and Gas, CNPC successfully bid in 2011 for a US$400m exploration licence to develop three oil blocks in the Amu Darya basin in northern Afghanistan. CNPC agreed to generous terms, including the construction of a refinery, a 15% royalty on oil, a 20% revenues tax and a 50% or more tax on

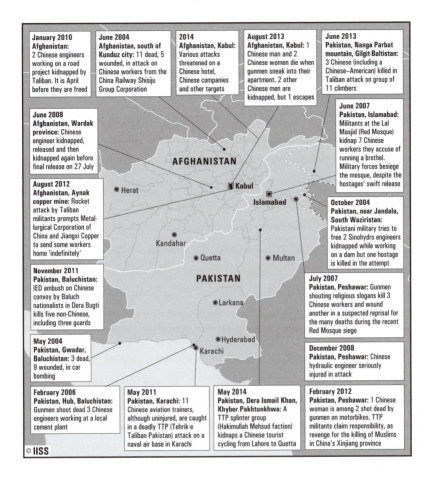

January 2010 Afghanistan: 2 Chinese engineers working on a road project kidnapped by Taliban. It is April before they are freed

June 2004 Afghanistan, south of Kunduz city: 11 dead, 5 wounded, in attack on Chinese workers from the China Railway Shisiju Group Corporation

2014 Afghanistan, Kabul: Various attacks threatened on a Chinese hotel, Chinese companies and other targets

August 2013 Afghanistan, Kabul: 1 Chinese man and 2 Chinese women die when gunmen sneak into their apartment. 2 other Chinese men are kidnapped, but 1 escapes

June 2013 Pakistan, Nanga Parbat mountain, Gilgit-Baltistan: 3 Chinese (including a Chinese–American) killed in Taliban attack on group of 11 climbers

June 2008 Afghanistan, Wardak province: Chinese engineer kidnapped, released and then kidnapped again before final release on 27 July

June 2007 Pakistan, Islamabad: Militants at the Lal Masjid (Red Mosque) kidnap 7 Chinese workers they accuse of running a brothel. Military forces besiege the mosque, despite the hostages' swift release

August 2012 Afghanistan, Aynak copper mine: Rocket attack by Taliban militants prompts Metallurgical Corporation of China and Jiangxi Copper to send some workers home 'indefinitely'

October 2004 Pakistan, near Jandala, South Waziristan: Pakistani military tries to free 2 Sinohydro engineers kidnapped while working on a dam but one hostage is killed in the attempt

November 2011 Pakistan, Baluchistan: IED ambush on Chinese convoy by Baluch nationalists in Dera Bugti kills five non-Chinese, including three guards

July 2007 Pakistan, Peshawar: Gunmen shouting religious slogans kill 3 Chinese workers and wound another in a suspected reprisal for the many deaths during the recent Red Mosque siege

May 2004 Pakistan, Gwadar, Baluchistan: 3 dead, 9 wounded, in car bombing

December 2008 Pakistan, Peshawar: Chinese hydraulic engineer seriously injured in attack

February 2006 Pakistan, Hub, Baluchistan: Gunmen shoot dead 3 Chinese engineers working at a local cement plant

May 2011 Pakistan, Karachi: 11 Chinese aviation trainers, although uninjured, are caught in a deadly TTP (Tehrik-e Taliban Pakistan) attack on a naval air base in Karachi

May 2014 Pakistan, Dera Ismail Khan, Khyber Pakhtunkhwa: A TTP splinter group (Hakimullah Mehsud faction) kidnaps a Chinese tourist cycling from Lahore to Quetta

February 2012 Pakistan, Peshawar: 1 Chinese woman is among 2 shot dead by gunmen on motorbikes. TTP militants claim responsibility, as revenge for the killing of Muslims in China's Xinjiang province

Map labels: AFGHANISTAN, PAKISTAN, Herat, Kabul, Islamabad, Kandahar, Quetta, Multan, Larkana, Hyderabad, Karachi

© IISS

profits, which could ultimately generate annual tax revenues of more than US$300m.[16] As most of the oil produced would go to the Afghan market, this first significant investment in the Afghan oil sector was also designed to assist Afghanistan's transition from an aid-dependent to a self-reliant economy.[17]

Yet, just as MCC had at Mes Aynak, CNPC found its engineers coming under threat in the Amu Darya basin. In 2012, reports surfaced that CNPC engineers were being harassed on site by men loyal to army chief of staff and Uzbek warlord General Abdul Rashid Dostum, leading to a break in construction.[18] When deciding to partner with Watan, CNPC found it could not avoid being drawn into Afghanistan's internal power rivalries. Watan Group is believed to be controlled by the family of former president Karzai and it owns a private security company, Watan Risk Management, which was awarded a US$7m contract to guard the Amu Darya basin oil project.[19] However, Watan has also been hit by scandal, having been accused of paying Taliban groups for safe passage when awarded a contract by the US to escort logistics convoys.[20] Its links to Karzai's tribes made it, as well as its Chinese partner CNPC, a target for Karzai's rival, Dostum.[21]

For all of China's pro-development rhetoric, Aynak and the Amu Darya basin have been about business interests and corporate strategy.[22] Chinese state-owned firms have entered Afghanistan bearing high levels of risk. Some Chinese experts even suspect that, in China's state-driven political economy, MCC gambled that it would be able to deliver a very generous package in a risky place because the Chinese state would be forced to come to its rescue.[23] CNPC's goal was more to establish a foothold in Afghanistan to take advantage of future regional growth in the energy market. Once on the ground in Afghanistan, however, Chinese firms have had to rethink their strategy, and their main response to trouble has been to freeze activities and repatriate personnel.

In 2009, Chinese experts put the number of Chinese residing in Afghanistan at approximately 1,000. Five years later, the number had probably dropped to fewer than 400.[24] Another source, a Chinese businessman back in Beijing after making a fortune in the Afghan steel business, has suggested that by 2013 fewer than 100 remained in the country.[25]

In 2013, trade between China and Afghanistan was valued at US$338m, a tiny percentage of the larger, US$9 trillion Chinese economy and clearly not enough of an incentive for Beijing to play a role in Afghan security.[26] Poor security conditions have prevented Chinese companies' greater involvement in the

Afghan economy, just as they have deterred Western firms. If China's economic footprint is to expand in Afghanistan, it will not be as part of a policy to foster peace and security, but rather only if stability is first guaranteed. In this regard, it appears symbolic that Afghanistan does not appear on maps of China's 'New Silk Road', a pet project of President Xi Jinping that plans to equip China with new trade routes to Europe and Africa. The land link envisaged runs from Xian in Shaanxi province, through Gansu province and Xinjiang, before traversing Central Asia into Iran, Turkey and beyond.[27]

China's reluctant involvement in Afghanistan

Yet despite the current commercial setbacks, longer-term strategic and security concerns have visibly affected Chinese foreign policy towards Afghanistan, in that it remains concerned about the protection of Chinese nationals in greater Central Asia (which includes both Afghanistan and Xinjiang).

For years, Chinese diplomacy on the protection of Chinese nationals was conducted in private and only revealed in public in vague terms, such as when the 2006 Treaty of Good-Neighbourly Friendship and Cooperation between Beijing and Kabul vowed to fight the 'three evils' (meaning terrorism, extremism and separatism).[28] However, the language has hardened under Chinese President Xi: a joint statement signed with President Karzai in 2013 mentions an Afghan 'readiness to take tangible measures to enhance the security of Chinese institutions and people in Afghanistan',[29] and when welcoming new Afghan President Ashraf Ghani to Beijing in October 2014, Xi underlined his personal 'hope that Afghanistan will continuously take effective measures to ensure safety of Chinese institutions and personnel'.[30]

Despite this, there remain serious limits to what a weak state like Afghanistan can achieve in providing security to Chinese nationals, and China has had to rely on its own agency and on law-enforcement cooperation with Afghanistan. Since the formation of the Snow Leopard Commando Unit of the People's Armed Police (PAP) in 2002, for example, personnel from that elite force have been sent to protect its diplomats in Kabul.[31]

One of the measures taken by Afghanistan was for the Ministry of Mines to establish a 'security perimeter' around the Aynak copper mine to discourage attacks.[32] After a visit to Kabul in September 2012 by then-Minister of Public Security Zhou Yongkang, the first trip by a Politburo Standing Committee member to Afghanistan in more than 40 years, an agreement was announced to send 300 Afghan police officers to China for training.[33] This was not the first Chinese offer of training; in July 2010, at the international conference on Afghanistan in Kabul, China's then-foreign minister, Yang Jiechi, disclosed that China had already trained 781 Afghan security person-nel.[34] Speaking at the Chinese embassy in Kabul in 2012, Zhou asked the diplomatic personnel there to stay safe, praising their work in Afghanistan as 'an enormous effort highly appreciated by the Chinese people and the motherland'.[35]

The day after President Xi welcomed President Ghani to Beijing in October 2014, China hosted the 'Heart of Asia Process', a multilateral conference initiated by Afghanistan to coordinate and deepen regional cooperation on economic and security issues. China started as an observer to this process in 2011, but has now moved centre stage by taking the significant step of hosting meetings. Beijing is involved in confidence-building discussions on counter-narcotics, disas-ter management and counter-terrorism but has stayed out of working groups on trade, education and regional infrastruc-tures.[36] The bilateral summit between the Chinese and Afghan presidents the day before reportedly led to more concrete assis-tance. However, the succession of two high-level diplomatic events confirmed that China was paying more attention to the security risks posed by Afghanistan's domestic security in light of the rapidly decreasing foreign military presence and doubts regarding the capacities of the Afghan police and military.

The same is evident in China's approach to the role of Shanghai Cooperation Organisation (SCO) in Afghanistan. With Chinese support, Afghanistan became an observer to the SCO in June 2012;[37] at the 2014 Dushanbe summit, China also supported the body's further enlargement. Although Pakistan, India and Iran are thought to be closer to membership, Afghanistan is a potential candidate. Some Chinese experts think that SCO membership can 'help Afghanistan to adjust to the right standards in terms of law-enforcement capacity'.[38] Afghanistan's engagement with the SCO helps intelligence cooperation, via the organisation's Tashkent-based Regional Anti-Terrorism Structure. However, beyond this concrete step and beyond the general sense that it supports regional engagement with Afghanistan, there is no clear road map of the role the SCO could play. Like other countries, China expressed support at the Dushanbe summit for an 'Afghan-led and Afghan-owned reconciliation and reconstruction process, so as to turn Afghanistan into a self-reliant and amicable nation'.[39]

China also took the unprecedented decision to facilitate talks between the Afghan government and various political factions, including the Taliban. In early 2015, China had hosted at least one such meeting with the Taliban in Beijing, possibly in the presence of Pakistani officials.[40]

In sum, while its main answer to the poor security situation has been to stay out of Afghanistan, China is nevertheless increasingly making limited contributions to building the country's capacity through engagement at a bilateral and a multilateral level, including supporting the peace process or economic-recovery projects. However, Chinese contributions will probably grow in size purely out of concern for the security of Chinese nationals in Afghanistan and for regional security. Its wish not to become a target and geopolitical concerns over regional competition with the US both continue to prevent China from taking a more holistic approach with higher-profile diplomacy. In 2009, China rejected US offers to play a role in Afghanistan. Some American requests were very specific, such as the opening of the Wakhan corridor – the eastern panhandle of Afghanistan that ends on the border with Xinjiang – in order to facilitate the logistics of military operations.[41] However, the only joint project by the US and China since 2012 has been in the training of Afghan diplomats.[42]

Nevertheless, China's low profile in the areas of peace and stability is changing as the international community draws down its troops in Afghanistan and the frequency of Xinjiang-related terrorist attacks in China increases. The protection of Chinese nationals, both overseas and within China, is clearly one of the main drivers of this shift.

Leaning on Pakistan for security assistance

Although both Chinese and Pakistani leaders like to refer to their two countries' close relationship as 'higher than the Karakorams, deeper than the oceans and sweeter than honey',[43] our collected data shows that Pakistan has been the most dangerous country for travelling Chinese nationals, with at least 12 Chinese killed in 11 separate attacks. This is not just a case of Chinese citizens being random victims of violence – even violence aimed at 'foreign' interests in general. Separatists in Pakistan's Baluchistan province have targeted two important Chinese projects in the region, the Gwadar port and the Saindak mine, for overtly political reasons.

The decades-old insurgency in Baluchistan is not linked to a radical religious agenda but to a nationalist movement, with one of its main demands for a greater share of the region's resources wealth. While Baluchistan produces 36% of Pakistan's natural gas, for example, it receives only 17% of output; and the Chinese presence has been used by the separatist Baluchistan Liberation Army to try to exert pressure on the central Pakistani government.[44]

In 2001, the Chinese government decided to help fund the first phase of the construction of a deep-water port on Baluchistan's Arabian Sea coast at Gwadar. China Harbour Engineering Company paid 80% of the US$250m construction bill for the initial facilities, which were delivered in 2006.[45] The Pakistani navy's ambitions to transform Gwadar into a major base fuelled suspicions in the US and India that the Chinese navy might have similar plans. Although there has been no hard evidence to support this contention, the rumours continue that Gwadar could become one of the first overseas Chinese naval bases, as part of what a US study called a 'string of pearls' strategy.[46]

However, the decision to build Gwadar came from Islamabad, angering many pro-independence Baluch groups. They complained of 'land grabs' by those associated with it and expressed concerns that an influx of outsiders to work on the project could alter the delicate demographic balance of the region.[47] As a result, they began targeting the port's construction.[48] In May 2004, for example, a car bomb exploded when a van belonging to China Harbour Engineering left for the port construction area, killing three Chinese staff.[49] The company persevered with the first phase of the port, but the security situation prevented Chinese involvement in the second stage. Although no more lives were lost, a series of attacks between 2004 and 2007 clearly targeted China Harbour Engineering.[50]

The cancellation of another ambitious Chinese project in Pakistan was announced in September 2011 by Kingho Group, one of China's largest private coal mining companies. Citing security concerns for its employees, Kingho revealed that it was pulling out from a US$19 billion deal in Singh province involving a coal mine as well as power and chemical plants.[51] In early 2015, Chinese oil-tanker drivers delivering fuel to the Saindak mine in the Chaghai hills were still being attacked and kidnapped.[52]

Such insecurity – and such risks for Chinese engineers and workers – has kept other projects in Pakistan on the drawing board. In February 2006, during a visit to Beijing, President Pervez Musharraf proposed a 'trade and energy corridor' linking Gwadar to Kashgar, the provincial capital of Xinjiang province. The plan was for a railroad from Gwadar, accompanied by gas and oil pipelines, plus an extension of the Karakoram Highway. This was meant to create a new strategic axis in western Asia, inexorably linking Pakistan and Xinjiang. The corridor would offer an alternative route for Chinese energy imports and exports of manufactured Pakistani products while associated projects would help Pakistan overcome its own energy-production crisis.

Yet very little has happened to advance the corridor project. Although the first phase of Gwadar has been successfully completed, traffic to the port remains significantly less than that to Karachi, as Gwadar has still not been connected to the Pakistani hinterland.[53] The government of Prime Minister Nawaz Sharif revived the idea of a corridor in July 2013 as an even more ambitious 'China–Pakistan economic corridor'.[54] According to Pakistani Minister for Planning and Development Ahsan Iqbal in 2014, this will include several energy, transportation and infrastructure projects worth more than US$35bn.[55] China now views the corridor as a southern leg of Xi Jinping's 'New Silk Road', linking the land-based belt to the Indian Ocean and the maritime route. Despite all this, rail, road and energy links from southwestern Pakistan to Xinjiang are still on the drawing board, although China has been funding road improvements along the Karakoram Highway from Kashgar almost to Islamabad.[56] In April 2015, during Xi's first state visit to Pakistan, the People's Bank of China announced US$1.7bn for the Karot hydropower project in Pakistan, as the first investment of China's new US$40bn New Silk Road fund. Karot is a key project of the China–Pakistan economic corridor.[57]

China may be more willing today than it was in 2011 to support economic cooperation with Pakistan, especially given the enormous political support in Beijing for a 'New Silk Road' through the region. Speaking in late 2014, a former Chinese diplomat based in Islamabad suggested that a combination of foreign-policy factors had led Beijing to reconsider the strategic value of relations with Islamabad. 'Strategic pressure in maritime East Asia is forcing us to look West; rebalancing East and West is part of our national security. In addition, we have more money to invest now in projects with Pakistan. And we have learned our lessons from the past. We need to move cautiously, step by step, taking the safety of our staff in consideration. But there is now a political will in Beijing that was lacking before.'[58]

That does not mean, however, that security concerns have evaporated. The Chinese ambassador to Pakistan, Sun Weidong, has explicitly called on the government in Islamabad to safeguard the security of Chinese staff during the construction of 'China–Pakistan economic corridor' projects.[59] However, unlike Afghanistan – and despite its own daunting domestic challenges – Pakistan has strong military, intelligence and law-enforcement capabilities on which China can rely in gradually expanding its economic presence in the country.

The Pakistani military intervention at Islamabad's Red Mosque (Lal Masjid) in 2007 was a case in point, showing the great lengths to which Pakistan was willing to go to sustain its friendship with China.[60] In June that year, radical students from the mosque abducted seven Chinese workers from a nearby 'health centre' near the mosque, accusing them of running a brothel. Although the hostages were soon released unharmed, China's Minister of Public Security Zhou Yongkang felt moved to raise 'for the umpteenth time' with his Pakistani counterpart the need to protect Chinese nationals working in Pakistan. In unusually frank remarks by Chinese standards, Zhou described the militants as 'terrorists' and demanded that Pakistan 'punish the criminals'.[61] His message was reinforced by PLA generals and President Hu Jintao in discussions with their Pakistani colleagues.[62]

While China generally follows a principle of discretion and low-key, closed-doors diplomacy when dealing with violent groups in third countries, it made an exception in the Red Mosque case. It encouraged and endorsed a decision by President Musharraf to launch a siege of the mosque. Beijing paid a price for being so vocal about its cause, because after hundreds of Pakistanis died in the storming of the mosque, three other Chinese nationals were shot dead in retaliation near Peshawar, in North West Frontier Province (now renamed Khyber Pakhtunkhwa).[63] However, some accounts suggested that China had linked the kidnappings to the influence of Uighur militants, and this would explain why it was so willing to go out on a limb.[64]

As the number of Chinese nationals has slowly grown in Pakistan – from 10,000 to 12,000 between 2009 and 2014 – the Pakistani government has offered increasingly formal assistance. In 2013, Xiong Lixin, vice-president of hydropower giant Sinohydro, mentioned that Chinese workers were being escorted to construction sites in Pakistan in helicopters with armed guards.[65] In 2014, Pakistan pledged 'army-backed security to big Chinese companies in the country to ensure their absolute protection'.[66]

Law-enforcement cooperation has also taken the form of special police units. In Lahore in June 2014, the municipal police established eight 'special security desks' for 'Chinese citizens employed in the government, semi-government and private sector as well as for tourists from China'.[67] The Communist Party office said at the time that all foreigners in the country, especially the Chinese, were on terrorists' hit lists, so providing security to them was of the utmost importance. A former Chinese diplomat in Islamabad later boasted that Beijing had an unusually good idea of the number of Chinese nationals in Pakistan. 'Chinese individuals want to benefit from the police protection of Pakistan, so they tend to signal their presence to our consular authorities.'[68]

In February 2015, Pakistani Minister for Planning and Development Iqbal went one step further, revealing in a press interview that Pakistan was training a special military unit to protect Chinese experts working on the China–Pakistan economic corridor.[69] When this project becomes reality, the number of Chinese in Pakistan is expected to further increase.[70]

In addition to government contacts, our earlier research has shown that China has had close exchanges with opposition parties, some of them Islamist, believing this could have a positive impact on the security of its nationals in Pakistan. In the long term, the aim is to sustain a united, pro-Chinese front among the Pakistani elite through the Chinese embassy in Islamabad and the International Liaison Department of the Communist Party. In 2009 and 2010, for instance, Beijing hosted representatives of Jamaat-e-Islami and Jamiat Ulema-e-Islam (JUI), two political parties with known links to fighters in Afghanistan, and in the case of JUI, with the Afghan and Pakistani Taliban.[71] As such, Pakistan provides a good example of China diversifying political contacts to secure its overseas interests.

Dealing with Islamist threats

While Chinese companies have let projects in Afghanistan and Pakistan languish because of the difficult security environment, these projects are in fact a less frequent target than works and civilians linked to the international military coalition in Afghanistan in the past decade. Taliban groups in Afghanistan and Pakistan have generally been more restrained in attacking Chinese interests.

However, in October 2009 a high-ranking al-Qaeda operative called on Uighurs to launch a jihad against Chinese 'infidels'. Abu Yahia al-Libi urged Uighurs to regain control over their land in Xinjiang, and retaliate against discriminatory Chinese policies.[72] This was a new development; al-Qaeda leaders had never previously pointed to China as a target.[73] A nightmare scenario for Beijing has been that politically motivated attacks originating in war zones in Afghanistan or the tribal areas of Pakistan should ripple out into Xinjiang or hit Chinese nationals and interests in Central Asia. The protection of nationals has therefore not only become an issue of preventing terrorist action inside Afghanistan and Pakistan, but also of containing contagion and spillover effects into China.

In the late 1990s, China relied on the offices of Pakistan to negotiate a deal with the Taliban government led by Mullah Omar. The resulting agreement included a promise by Afghanistan to monitor Uighur militants and not to permit hostile activities against Chinese interests.[74]

Today, similarly informal agreements are apparently being sought with the Taliban operating in and out of Pakistan, although the movement has become too diversified, and part of it is fighting the Pakistani state. In early 2015, we heard reports, only unofficially confirmed, that China had hosted a meeting in Beijing with representatives of Taliban factions, the Afghan government and Pakistani intelligence.[75] China's special envoy for Afghanistan, Ambassador Sun Yuxi, has said in public that his government was ready to 'welcome the Taliban in a neutral venue such as China' if the process was 'Afghan-led' and aimed at promoting peace in Afghanistan.[76] Such statements reinforce persistent rumours that China has always maintained contacts with the Taliban, often through Pakistani intelligence.[77] The main focus of Chinese requests has been on locating Uighur fighters in Afghanistan, and Beijing is still pursuing, so far successfully, the extradition from Afghanistan of Uighurs suspected of planning attacks.[78]

At the same time, some in China acknowledge that Western military operations in Afghanistan have indirectly benefited the protection of Chinese nationals. During a decade of war, the ranks of Uighur militants have faced attrition both within Afghanistan and in Pakistan's tribal areas. Many fighters were killed in the 2001 bombing of Tora Bora, and Uighur leader Hasan Mahsum was shot dead by the Pakistani army in South Waziristan in October 2003. Abu Yayha al-Libi, the al-Qaeda leader who directly threatened the Chinese in Xinjiang in 2009, died in a US drone strike in June 2012.[79] Today, there remain approximately 250 Uighur militants in Afghanistan, and fewer than 400 in Pakistan's North Waziristan province.[80] This weakening of the potential of Uighur militants to carry out attacks against China was a result of Pakistani support and a collateral benefit of US military operations.

Considering a higher profile

Afghanistan and Pakistan have clearly demonstrated that it is sometimes impossible even for China to decouple economic and security issues. Chinese firms have often fared better in hostile environments than their Western competitors, helped enormously by the fact that they have historically been less of a target for local resentment and radical groups. Such is the level of insecurity in Afghanistan and Pakistan, however, that it has strictly limited Chinese firms' movement. As a result, the protection of Chinese citizens in the region has become a top diplomatic priority for China, because of the potential for violence to spill over from its neighbours into its own territory.

Beijing's approach is different in each of the countries. In Afghanistan, where the apparatus of the state is weak, there is clearly a slow move towards greater engagement. China has made nascent contributions to training Afghan police and diplomats. Beijing's hosting of the 2014 Heart of Asia meeting and its mediation efforts in Afghan-led reconciliation are other indicators of this shift.

In Pakistan, although security is still poor, China can rely on the capacity of the state to protect its nationals and interests. While the support of the Pakistani police and military does not entirely eliminate the high risk of investing in Pakistan, it allows for slightly greater economic engagement and prospects for future growth. Pakistan could take advantage of Xi Jinping's ambitious 'New Silk Road' plans, as the only country able to connect the land route to the maritime route, from Kashgar to Gwadar. As such, Pakistan will be a test of China's resolve to carry out ambitious infrastructure plans in a complex security environment.

Chinese diplomacy has to walk a fine line, making it possible to protect Chinese nationals in Afghanistan and Pakistan without attracting the attention of Islamist groups. In both countries, China has paid special attention to maintaining a communication channel to radical groups. China is one of the very few countries that have consistently advocated talks with the Afghan Taliban, and it has both relied on its special relationship with Pakistan to reach out to them and has developed its own contacts to guard against the Taliban forging ties with Chinese militant Uighurs. This marked a significant departure from China's usual practice of speaking only with legitimate government authorities, one of the key features of its non-interference principle. In sum, Afghanistan and Pakistan have tested two core beliefs of China's foreign policy: the stabilising role of economic development and the focus of diplomacy on official state-to-state channels.

Notes

1   The Chinese refer to the concept of 'greater' Central Asia encompassing Afghanistan, Pakistan, Xinjiang and the five Central Asian republics: Kazakhstan, Kyrgyzstan, Tajikistan, Turkmenistan and Uzbekistan.

2   MFA, 'Statement by Yang Jiechi Minister of Foreign Affairs of the People's Republic of China At the High-level Meeting of the Security Council On Preventive Diplomacy', 26 September 2011, accessed at http://www.fmprc. gov.cn/mfa_eng/topics_665678/ yangjiechi_un_665740/t862325. shtml.

3   'China willing to spend big on Afghan commerce', *New York Times*, 29 December 2009.

4   *Ibid.*

5   'China's MCC turns back on US$3b Mes Aynak Afghanistan mine deal', *South China Morning Post*, 21 March 2014.

6   Steven Zyck, 'The role of China in Afghanistan's economic development and reconstruction', Civil–Military Fusion Centre, March 2012, accessed at http:// reliefweb.int/sites/reliefweb.int/ files/resources/Full_Report_3590. pdf.

7   World Bank, 'Q&A: Aynak and Mining in Afghanistan', 2 April 2013, accessed at http://www.worldbank.org/ en/news/feature/2013/04/02/ qa-aynak-mining-afghanistan.

8   James Brazier, 'Afghanistan Promises Tighter Security at Chinese-Run Mine', IHS Global Insight, 11 July 2012.

9   'Copper Bottomed? Bolstering the Aynak contract: Afghanistan's first major mining deal', Global Witness, November 2012, accessed at https://www. globalwitness.org/documents/.../ copper%20bottomed.pdf.

10 Michael Georgy, 'Chinese return to Afghan mine project – minister', Reuters, 29 November 2012.

11 'Chinese workers in Mes Aynak have warned to quit working on the site', Wadsam Afghan Business News Portal, 18 June 2013.

12 'China's MCC turns back on US$3b Mes Aynak Afghanistan mine deal', *South China Morning Post*.

13 Emma Graham-Harrison, 'Mes Aynak highlights Afghanistan's dilemma over protecting heritage', *Guardian*, 23 May 2013.

14 'China pledges assistance to Afghanistan', Xinhua, 28 October 2014.

15 'MCC asked to resume work on copper project', *Pajhwok Afghan News*, 8 December 2014.

16 Zyck, 'The role of China in Afghanistan's economic development and reconstruction'.

17 'China's CNPC begins oil production in Afghanistan', Reuters, 21 October 2012.

18 'Missing refinery deal halts landmark China–Afghan oil project', Reuters, 18 August 2013.

19 Afghan Watan Risk Management, accessed at http://watanrisk.com/experience.php.

20 'US cuts off Afghan firm', *Wall Street Journal*, 8 December 2010.

21 'Hamid Karzai government under fire for oil deal with company run by cousin', *Telegraph*, 20 June 2012.

22 Erica Downs, 'China buys into Afghanistan', *SAIS Review of International Affairs*, vol. 32, no. 2, Summer–Fall 2012, pp. 65–84.

23 Senior policy analyst, Author interview, Beijing, November 2013.

24 Academics, experts and retired diplomats, Author interviews, Chengdu, November 2009 and October 2014.

25 'China's dilemma in Afghanistan', *South China Morning Post*, 5 December 2013.

26 MFA, 'Afghanistan country profile', accessed at http://www.fmprc.gov.cn/mfa_chn/gjhdq_603914/gj_603916/yz_603918/1206_603920/.

27 'China to establish $40 billion Silk Road infrastructure fund', Reuters, 8 November 2014. For details on the New Silk Road, see 'China's Initiatives on Building Silk Road Economic Belt and 21st-century Maritime Silk Road', Xinhua, available at http://www.xinhuanet.com/english/special/silkroad/.

28 'Joint Statement between China and Afghanistan', Beijing, 21 June 2006, accessed at http://english.people.com.cn/200606/21/eng20060621_275755.html. During the discussions that led to the signing of a strategic partnership between Beijing and Kabul in 2012, the 'three evils' were again the coded phrase encapsulating Chinese security concerns; see 'Zhongguo yu Afuhan jianli zhanlüe hezuo huoban guanxi lianye xuanyan' (China and Afghanistan: Joint Declaration on Strategic Partnership: full text), China News Network, 8 June 2012, accessed at http://www.chinanews.com/gn/2012/06-08/3948964.shtml.

29 MFA, 'Joint Statement on Deepening Strategic and Cooperative Partnership, Beijing', 30 September 2013, accessed at http://mfa.gov.af/en/news/joint-statement-between-the-islamic-republic-of-afghanistan-and-the-peoples-republic-of-china-on-deepening-strategic-and-cooperative-partnership.

30 MFA, 'Xi Jinping Holds Talks with President Ashraf Ghani of Afghanistan, Stressing China Values Developing China–Afghanistan Strategic Cooperative Partnership and Hopes Afghanistan Achieve

Enduring Peace and Stable Development', 28 October 2014, accessed at http://www.fmprc.gov.cn/mfa_eng/zxxx_662805/t1205547.shtml.

31 'Xuebao tuji dui baohu woguo Afuhan shiguan' (Snow Leopard special units protect Chinese Embassy in Afghanistan), Sina.com, 23 August 2009, accessed at http://news.sina.com.cn/w/2009-08-23/064416169594s.shtml.

32 World Bank, 'Q&A: Aynak and Mining in Afghanistan', 2 April 2013.

33 'Security chief's Afghan visit captures attention of world media', Sina.com, 24 September 2012.

34 'Yang Jiechi 20 ri chu Afuhan wenti guoji huiyi bing fabiao jianghua' (July 20: Yang Jiechi attends an international conference on Afghanistan and delivers a speech), , State Council of China, 21 July 2010, accessed at http://www.gov.cn/jrzg/2010-07/21/content_1659784.htm.

35 'Zhou Yongkang tongzhi kanwang weiwen Zhongguo zhu Afuhan shiguan gongzuo renyuan ji zhongzi jigou daibiao' (Comrade Zhou Yongkang greets personnel of Chinese Embassy in Afghanistan and representatives of Chinese companies), Embassy of the PRC in Afghanistan, 25 September 2012, accessed at http://af.china-embassy.org/chn/sgxw/t972951.htm.

36 Richard Ghiasy and Maihan Saeedi, 'The Heart of Asia Process at a Juncture: An analysis of Impediments to Further Progress', Afghan Institute for International Studies Policy Paper, Kabul, June 2014.

37 'Hu Jintao yu Afuhan zongtong huitan cheng fengxing dui a youhao zhengce' (Hu Jintao in meeting with Afghan counterpart says China will pursue friendly policy), Xinhua, 8 June 2012, accessed at http://world.huanqiu.com/roll/2012-06/2799601.html.

38 Senior Chinese academic, Author interview, Chengdu, October 2014.

39 'SCO members support Afghan-led reconciliation process', China Daily, 12 September 2014.

40 'Pakistanis try to nudge Taliban along the path of peace talks with Kabul', New York Times, 18 February 2015.

41 Academics, experts and former diplomats, Author interviews, Beijing and Chengdu, 2009 and 2014.

42 'Opening Ceremony of U.S.–China Joint Training Program for Afghan Diplomats', US Embassy Beijing, 16 May 2014, accessed at http://beijing.usembassy-china.org.cn/2014ir/opening-ceremony-of-u.s.-china-joint-training-program-for-afghan-diplomats.html.

43 See, e.g., Mushahid Hussain Sayed, 'Pakistan–China Relations: strategic partners in the 21st century', Pakistan–China Institute, 29 May 2012.

44 Mathieu Duchâtel, 'The Terrorist Risk and China's Policy towards Pakistan: Strategic reassurance and the "United Front"', Journal of Contemporary China, vol. 20, no. 71 (September 2011), pp. 543–61.

45 Andrew Small, The China–Pakistan Axis: Asia's New Geopolitics (C.

Hurst & Co. Publishers: London, 2015), pp. 100–03.

46 The first study to use the term was 'Energy futures in Asia', a leaked Booz Allen Hamilton report for US Defense Secretary Donald Rumsfeld; see 'China builds up strategic sea lanes', *Washington Times*, 17 January 2005. For more on the strategy, see Christopher J. Pehrson, 'String of Pearls': Meeting the challenge of China's rising power across the Asian littoral', Strategic Studies Institute, US Army War College, July 2006. For a Chinese perspective, see Zhou Bo, 'The String of Pearls and the Maritime Silk Road', *China US Focus*, 11 February 2014, accessed at http://www.chinausfocus.com/foreign-policy/the-string-of-pearls-and-the-maritime-silk-road/.

47 International Crisis Group, 'Pakistan: The Worsening Conflict in Balochistan', Asia Report No. 119, September 2006, p. 15.

48 Kiyya Baloch, 'Can China's Gwadar Port Dream Survive Local Ire?', *Diplomat*, 17 December 2014.

49 '3 engineers killed in car bomb in Pakistan', *China Daily*, 3 May 2004.

50 Small, *The China–Pakistan Axis: Asia's New Geopolitics*, p. 102

51 'China Pullout Deals Blow to Pakistan', *Wall Street Journal*, 30 September 2011.

52 Kiyya Baloch, 'Chinese Operations in Balochistan Again Targeted by Militants', *Diplomat*, 27 March 2015.

53 Syed Fazl-e-Haider, 'Insurgency stunts Gwadar progress', *Asia Times*, 9 May 2014.

54 'Projects prioritized in the China–Pakistan economic corridor', Chinese government, 9 July 2014, accessed at http://www.china.org.cn/business/2014-07/09/content_32901466.htm.

55 'Sino–Pakistan economic corridor a boon: Minister', *Global Times*, 9 July 2014.

56 Hasnain Kazim, 'The Karakoram Highway: China's Asphalt Powerplay in Pakistan', *Spiegel*, 17 July 2012.

57 'China's Silk Road Fund makes first investment in Pakistan's hydropower project', Xinhua, 21 April 2015.

58 Senior academic, Author interview, Chengdu, October 2014.

59 John C.K. Daly, 'India unsettled by proposed China–Pakistan economic corridor through Kashmir', *China Brief* (Jamestown Foundation), vol. 14, no. 5, 6 March 2014.

60 As President Musharraf said at the time, 'The Chinese, who are such great friends of ours – they took the Chinese hostage and tortured them. Because of this, I was personally embarrassed. I had to go apologise to the Chinese leaders', quoted in Peter Lee, 'ISIS tentacles reach towards China', *Asia Times*, 15 August 2014.

61 Those claiming responsibility said the murders were a reprisal for China's endorsement of Islamabad's decision to storm the mosque; see 'Lal Masjid damage to Pak–China relations', *Daily Times*, 29 June 2007.

62 For a detailed account of the Red Mosque events, see Small, *The*

China–Pakistan Axis: Asia's New Geopolitics, pp. ix–xvi.

63 Lee, 'ISIS tentacles reach towards China'.

64 Small, *The China–Pakistan Axis: Asia's New Geopolitics*, p. xiv.

65 'Security fears hinder Chinese projects in Pakistan', *Hindu*, 9 August 2013.

66 'Chinese companies to get army-backed security in Pakistan', Xinhua, 3 March 2014.

67 'Special desks set up to provide security to Chinese citizens', *Tribune*, 15 June 2014.

68 Senior academic, Author interview, Chengdu, October 2014.

69 'Pakistan raising special force to protect Chinese experts', *News International* (Pakistan), 22 February 2015.

70 'Overseas Chinese in Pakistan laud national day parade in Beijing', *People's Daily*, 1 October 2009; and 'Footprints, the Chinese Pakistan', *Dawn*, 18 April 2014.

71 Duchâtel, 'The Terrorist Risk and China's Policy towards Pakistan', pp. 552–53.

72 *Ibid.*

73 'Al-Qaeda leader Abu Yahia Al-Libi killed in US drone strike', *Telegraph*, 5 June 2012.

74 Andrew Small, 'Afghanistan, the view from China', EU Institute for Strategic Studies, January 2014, accessed at http://www.iss.europa.eu/uploads/media/Alert_6_Afghanistan_China.pdf.

75 Academics, experts and former diplomats, Author interviews, Beijing, Shanghai and Chengdu, January 2015.

76 Ahmed Rashid, 'Viewpoint: Can China bring peace to Afghanistan?', BBC News, 1 December 2014.

77 Small, *The China–Pakistan Axis: Asia's New Geopolitics*, p. 142.

78 Bethany Matta, 'China to neighbours: Send us your Uighurs', Al Jazeera, 18 February 2015.

79 Duchâtel, 'The Terrorist Risk and China's Policy towards Pakistan', p. 548.

80 'From his Pakistan hideout, Uighur leader vows revenge on China', Reuters, 14 March 2014.

CHAPTER FOUR

Murder on the Mekong: The long arm of Chinese law

The murder of 13 Chinese sailors on the Mekong River in October 2011 prompted a technically still non-interventionist Beijing to become de facto a river cop along Southeast Asia's longest waterway. '10/5', as it is sometimes called in China,[1] was one of the largest attacks on Chinese nationals outside the country. As such, it required a robust response by the Chinese government. Before the case was closed, this involved an unprecedented law-enforcement operation abroad, the first Chinese trial of foreigners for alleged crimes against Chinese citizens overseas, and the first contemplation by Beijing of a targeted drone strike.

The Mekong (Lancang in Chinese) flows south from China through the notorious 'Golden Triangle' on the borders of Myanmar, Laos and Thailand, before continuing through Cambodia and Vietnam into the sea. The river bustles with small ships carrying a growing volume of legitimate goods. But since the lawless Golden Triangle is one of the world's prime drugs-producing regions – second only to Afghanistan – the Mekong is also a major smuggling route.

On 5 October 2011, near the Thai river port of Chiang Saen, two Chinese-crewed barges, the *Hua Ping* and *Yu Xing*

8, were fired upon and those on board brutally killed. Among the ships' cargo of apples and garlic, Thai military officials from the elite anti-narcotics Pha Muang task force discovered 920,000 'yaba' methamphetamine pills with an estimated street value of US$3 million.[2] Accounts of the incident differ, but initial reports suggested a gunfight between police and drug traffickers who had hijacked the ship in order to smuggle the pills into Thailand. The Pha Muang pointed the finger of blame for the hijacking at ethnic Shan drug trafficker Naw Kham and his criminal gang.[3]

One sailor was found dead on the *Hua Ping*. The incident provoked shock and outrage among the Chinese public two days later when the bodies of other murdered crew members washed up on the Thai shores of the river. Their swollen, waterlogged bodies showed signs of gunshot and other injuries – including a broken neck. Most of them were blindfolded and had their hands tied behind their backs, pointing to execution-style killings.

Four days after the attack, on Monday in Beijing, Chinese Ministry of Foreign Affairs (MFA) spokesman Liu Weimin confirmed the deaths of 11 Chinese sailors. Two other missing sailors were later found dead. Liu also announced that Yunnan, the nearest Chinese province, had 'suspended operation of Chinese passenger and cargo ships on the Mekong River' and added that his ministry had asked the governments of Thailand, Laos and Myanmar to 'take effective measures to protect Chinese ships and crewmen'.[4] Yunnan dispatched a working group to Thailand to coordinate with local authorities. The MFA's Liu also mentioned that the case had the attention of the Chinese leadership.[5]

During the crisis in Libya earlier in 2011, Chinese internet users had forcefully urged Beijing to protect its citizens and criticised it for not moving faster.[6] Now, as grisly pictures of the dead sailors circulated online, strong feelings were again expressed in the Chinese blogosphere. Hundreds of thousands commented on microblogging site Weibo, the Chinese equivalent of Twitter. 'The authorities owe justice to the people, especially the killed people and their relatives,' was a typical reaction from one Chinese netizen.[7] Meanwhile, the nationalistic *Global Times* ran an editorial lambasting the Thai authorities' handling of the case. The newspaper insisted that 'China should take full part in the investigation', and urged 'relevant countries to launch a powerful strike on those responsible'.[8] Chinese public pressure was growing on the government to act swiftly and decisively.

Beijing swings into action

China had both political and economic reasons to act. In 2001, an agreement began between Beijing and neighbouring countries to expand trade and shipping on the river. In that first year, the annual volume of goods transported along the waterway was estimated at just 500 tonnes.[9] By 2010, however, the river had become an efficient conduit for delivering Chinese goods to Thailand's lucrative markets and total trade had soared to 300,000 tonnes.[10]

The majority of international shipping on the Mekong is Chinese, and while the attack on the *Hua Ping* and *Yu Xing 8* was uncommonly bloody and happened in broad daylight, it was far from the first incident. In April 2011, for example, Naw Kham's gang had hijacked three boats taking goods to a Chinese-owned casino on the Laotian side of the river across from Chiang Saen. Zhao Wei, the owner of the Kings Romans Casino, was forced to pay a 25m THB (US$733,000) ransom for the safe return of the ships and their crews.[11]

The decision by the Yunnan government to suspend Chinese maritime traffic on the Mekong in the wake of the October 2011 killings left 164 Chinese sailors on 28 ships stranded in Chiang Saen, the Thai estuary gateway to the Golden Triangle.[12]

Eight days after the killings, several Chinese patrol vessels were dispatched to Thailand by Yunnan's border police – a provincial arm of the Ministry of Public Security (MPS) – to escort these stranded Chinese ships safely home. This deployment through Burmese and Laotian waters prefigured an increased security role for China on the Mekong.

Meanwhile, an investigative team composed of officials from China's ministries of foreign affairs, public security and transport began examining the *Hua Ping* and *Yu Xing 8* in Chiang Saen. Guo Shaochun, the MFA official heading the team and in charge of cooperation with Thai authorities, acknowledged the public pressure for results. 'The Chinese people, leaders and media are greatly concerned over the investigation of the attack,' he said, adding that Chinese and Thai authorities were 'obliged' to solve the case and bring the killers to justice.[13]

In Beijing, Vice Foreign Minister Song Tao called in the Thai, Lao and Burmese envoys to demand more cooperation from their countries in capturing the culprits. Instead of China's typical behind-the-scenes approach, these diplomatic meetings were made public, probably due to the widespread popular interest.[14]

With newspaper editorials turning up the volume, talking about 'rights to launch countermeasures against the killing of Chinese citizens', security officials began to take the baton from their softer-spoken colleagues in foreign affairs.[15] On 15 October, Vice Minister of Public Security Zhang Xinfeng led a delegation to Bangkok to speed up the process of finding the perpetrators and bringing them to justice. Eight days later, Minister of Public Security Meng Jianzhu publicly exhorted Thailand, Laos and Myanmar to get to the bottom of the case.[16] The MPS was now clearly spearheading efforts, even though the murders were committed outside China.

Concern to catch the perpetrators also gradually percolated to the top. Later in October, Chinese Defence Minister Liang Guanglie offered Laotian Deputy Prime Minister and Defence Minister Douangchay Phichit Chinese military support 'if necessary'.[17] Meanwhile, Premier Wen Jiabao telephoned Thai leader Yingluck Shinawatra to push the case for joint law enforcement along the Mekong River.[18]

A *China Daily* editorial had already suggested the massacre 'should be taken as a clarion call for forming a transnational security mechanism at a sub-regional level so that drug trafficking and other organized crimes can be rigorously eradicated in the area and personnel and cargo safety along the Mekong can be guaranteed'.[19] The *Global Times* predicted that: 'The proper settlement of this tragedy will test the Chinese government's ability to protect its overseas interests, and may reshape China's stake in the region.'[20] An article in Shanghai's *Oriental Morning Post* even suggested that China should 'station its own police force directly' in the region and take a role in training Burmese and Lao forces.[21]

Clearly, Chinese politicians were thinking along the same lines when they urged their three neighbours to attend a summit on 31 October to establish a law-enforcement cooperation mechanism along the Mekong to deal with the 'new security situation on the river'.[22] The immediate priority, however, was to bring those behind the brutal massacre to justice.

The hunt for the perpetrators

In what was now shaping up as a political thriller, doubts had been cast on the first official accounts of the 10/5 Mekong River attack. Members of Thailand's Pha Muang military task force initially said they had boarded the ships after they were moored in Chiang Saen. On 28 October, however, nine Pha Muang service personnel were themselves brought before police in the northern Thai city of Chiang Rai and accused of complicity in the murders and of tampering with evidence.

Liu Yuejin, the director of the Narcotics Control Bureau within the Chinese MPS, travelled to the region to coordinate the search for the killers, and more than 200 Chinese police were involved in a multinational investigation. Chinese police 'actively cooperated' with their Thai, Lao and Burmese counterparts, sharing intelligence about Naw Kham and his gang; they also swept the region and facilitated joint clean-up operations. Li Zhuqun, a senior police officer, explained that 'We sent police to Laos and Myanmar to carry out interrogations, and exchanged evidence with Thailand.'[23]

Nevertheless, poor knowledge of the local terrain and the need to protect locals meant that it took until April 2012 before Naw Kham was apprehended.

In December 2011, Chinese media reported that Chinese officers were participating in a raid in Boqiao province in Laos designed to capture the semi-legendary gang leader. Tipped off by villagers, Naw Kham escaped to his usual base of Talichek in neighbouring Myanmar, but his mistress and gang members were captured and weapons seized. In Myanmar, the Chinese police found it difficult to continue the pursuit, not because of a question of jurisdiction but 'because of the dense forest and complex terrain', according to one participating Chinese police officer, Ma Jun.[24] In February 2012, a joint Chinese and Burmese police team raided Naw Kham's hideout, but he once again evaded capture.

Four months into the manhunt, and with significant public pressure on the Chinese government to secure arrests, the MPS apparently began to consider unorthodox methods. Liu Yuejin revealed in an interview with the *Global Times* that 'one plan was to use an unmanned aircraft to carry 20 kilograms of TNT to bomb the area' in Myanmar where Naw Kham was suspected to be hiding.[25] This step was never taken, but would have marked a new beginning, a decisive break from China's policy of non-interference.

It remains unclear how serious the plan ever was. One weapons expert interviewed by the *New York Times* suggested China may have prevaricated because of a lack of confidence in its untested technology. Liu himself said the plan was abandoned because the order was to catch Naw Kham alive. He also admitted that China's use of a drone for this purpose 'would have met with problems' and that the pullback was related 'to international and sovereignty issues'.[26]

A show trial for Naw Kham

Two months later, the net finally closed around Naw Kham when investigators learned the drug kingpin was planning to slip back into Laos. Chinese security chief Liu alerted his Laotian counterparts, who were there to capture the fugitive late in the evening of 25 April 2012.

Naw Kham's capture was 'a hard-nosed display' of China's 'political and economic clout across Laos, Myanmar and Thailand'[27] – demonstrating that the long arm of Chinese law reached beyond the country's boundaries – and his subsequent trial and execution in China were a show of the country's new-found capacity to mete out justice for crimes against overseas Chinese interests.

When the chief suspect arrived in Kunming on a chartered plane from the Laotian capital, Vientiane, he was escorted down the steps in handcuffs by heavily armed police before the waiting media. Much of the three-day trial in September was, unusually, broadcast live, with China Central Television airing a clip several days beforehand purporting to show Naw Kham confessing – although there are questions about the translation of his words into Mandarin Chinese.[28]

The gang leader and five accomplices were charged with homicide, kidnapping and drug trafficking. The prosecution case, as articulated by the deputy director of the Yunnan Provincial Public Security Bureau, Xian Yanming, was that: 'Naw Kham's criminal gang colluded with renegade Thai soldiers in premeditated attacks on Chinese ships. ... Naw Kham's group would hijack Chinese cargo ships, conceal drugs on board to frame the crew and then send them into Thai waters to make it appear that the authorities had uncovered a major drug-related case and killed the "drug traffickers". Meanwhile, Naw Kham's drug-trafficking ships would have unimpeded passage through Thai waters.'[29]

The trial broke new legal ground in having Thai police and 13 other witnesses from Thailand and Laos appear in court.[30] Thai Deputy Prime Minister Chalerm Yubamrung confirmed that country had 'worked closely with Chinese authorities in this case and provided all evidence to the Chinese side'.[31]

However, only three of the defendants admitted to have been present during the attack on the *Hua Ping* and *Yu Xing 8*, and witness testimonies left further questions about the official version of events. In court, Naw Kham was seen to deny being with his henchmen on the river that day, although Xinhua later reported that he had pleaded guilty.

Forensic evidence, though inconclusive, pointed to the Chinese sailors having been killed with Thai military-issue weapons.[32] Various hypotheses supposed that the Pha Muang task force had planted the drugs themselves and were using Naw Kham as a scapegoat, had tried to plant the drugs themselves but met resistance from the Chinese sailors, or were trying to steal the drugs. A Thai parliamentary committee later concluded that Thai officials were at least involved in the sailors' deaths. Other sources suggest that the Chinese sailors might also have been involved in trafficking.[33]

Throughout, however, China sought to portray the proceedings as free and fair, with due defence and simultaneous translation provided for the defendants. And whatever the uncertainties or competing theories, Naw Kham and three of his accomplices were found guilty and subsequently sentenced to death.

In an unsuccessful Supreme Court appeal, Naw Kham made a last-minute bid to insist on his innocence. 'The crime was carried out by the Thais,' he contended. 'I only got to know about it through television.' Shortly afterwards, on 1 March 2013, he and his accomplices were executed by lethal injection, with the proceedings again aired live on state television right up until the administration of the fatal dose. Shi Yinhong, a well-known intellectual based at Beijing's Renmin University, explained that the broadcast was meant to underline the government's capacity to protect Chinese citizens both inside and outside the country.[34]

It seems that Naw Kham's execution assuaged Chinese broader public anger. 'I have been waiting for this day for a long time,' declared Yang Xueguang, the father of one of the victims.[35] Liu Yuejin, the man who directed Beijing's law-enforcement operations, hailed the case as an example of 'the Chinese government's right to protect the legitimate interests and rights of Chinese citizens overseas'. In early 2015, the Thai soldiers implicated in the case still hadn't been officially charged. The judge in Naw Kham's case had also ordered those convicted to pay 6m RMB (US$960,000) in compensation to the victims' families.[36]

Joint patrols expand China's influence

The capture of Naw Kham and the break-up of his gang was bound to make the Mekong River safer for commercial traffic. Statistics from the Yunnan Provincial Public Security Bureau show that the gang was alone responsible for 28 attacks on Chinese ships between 2008 and 2011.[37] It also extorted protection money from boats plying the river. However, even as the murder investigation was still unfolding, Beijing was looking for a wider, longer-term solution.

The leading role played by the MPS was underlined by the fact that it was Zhou Yongkang – then one of the top five Communist Party leaders and ultimately in charge of public security – who convened the top-level gathering on the Mekong River on 31 October with counterparts from Myanmar, Laos and Thailand. The most far-reaching measure agreed under the 'Law Enforcement Cooperation along the Mekong River Mechanism' signed at the end of the meeting was to establish joint river patrols, particularly between Guanlei in Yunnan and Chiang Saen in Thailand. Another outcome of the meeting was a combined police operations centre in the Guanlei port of Xishuangbanna for coordination and intelligence sharing. China also pledged to help build the policing capacity of Burma and Laos.

China initially proposed joint river patrols, perhaps seeing these as a logical extension of its earlier mission to escort home ships stranded in Thailand after the suspension of Chinese maritime traffic on the Mekong in October. However, Thailand was wary from the outset of allowing Chinese vessels into its territorial waters, saying that this would require Thai parliamentary approval. Instead, the four nations approved coordinated river patrols, in which police vessels would travel to their country's riparian borders before handing over to counterparts on the other side.[38]

Vice-Minister of Public Security Meng Hongwei attended the founding ceremony of the combined operations centre and the establishment of a special Chinese unit dedicated to patrol and rescue operations. China initially dispatched five ships and 200 police officers to the mission from the China Border Police Force, including heavily armed special troops according to photos released by the Chinese military.[39]

Joint patrols began in December 2011 and before the sixth patrol set out in August 2012, unit commander Zhu Dezhong reported that 89 ships had been escorted, protecting 147 sailors from possible hijackers. By March 2015, 32 joint patrols, including escort, inspections and interception, had been conducted.[40]

Over time, the Chinese have gradually pushed the boundaries of the patrol mission. For example, in September 2012, an official with the patrol unit said that China and Laos had agreed to expand cooperation from the river to key spots on land, thus extending China's capacity to respond even on selected areas of Lao territory.[41] That seemed to have been prompted by practical necessity. In the middle of January 2012, a Chinese cargo ship came under fire from bandits on the Lao side and a patrol ship came to the rescue and returned fire.[42] China also took the lead in setting up an intercom system for boats to report attacks in real time through Beidou, China's GPS equivalent, although it is unclear whether the intercom system is actually working.[43]

The Mekong's new river cop?

The Mekong initiative is 'another indication of Beijing's growing influence in the region and its willingness to utilize its security forces to protect Chinese economic interests and citizens abroad'.[44] However, as with its protective missions in Afghanistan, Pakistan, Libya and Sudan, Beijing's deeper engagement in the Golden Triangle was not the result of any grand strategy, but rather a reaction to events and an improvised, evolving response to public calls to protect Chinese citizens and interests abroad.

The case did break new ground in bringing foreigners before a Chinese court for crimes committed against Chinese people overseas. Chief investigator Liu observed, 'The murders happened overseas. All the investigations, arrests and evidence collection were carried out outside China, and all the suspects were foreigners. That's unprecedented in the history of the Chinese police.'[45]

Despite China's much-vaunted principle of non-interference in other states' affairs, the Chinese public seems pleased with such developments. *China Youth Daily*, the Communist Youth League newspaper, applauded a 'successful example' of protecting 'the legitimate rights and interests of overseas Chinese citizens'. Although all of the events occurred outside China's borders, the paper concluded that 'our country has unquestionable jurisdiction'.[46] He Jingjun, a professor from Chongqing, further claimed that Naw Kham's execution was 'a milestone in China's protection of citizens overseas' and said China should continue to build an 'economic and financial sanctions protection net to deal a heavy blow to those foreign criminal organizations trampling on the rights of Chinese citizens'.[47]

Perhaps it was inevitable that Chinese security operations would follow vital Chinese economic interests in such an anarchic region as the Golden Triangle, where the law-enforcement capacity of its neighbours is much weaker than Beijing's. However, China's swift realisation that it needed a longer-term, not just a one-off, solution is also interesting. The patrols on the Mekong River have been established under a regular multilateral framework, creating a new 'security model' as the *Beijing Times* newspaper has put it. Just as anti-drug cooperation brought US law enforcement into Mexico and Latin America, this latest move is expanding China's role as a great power, drawing it into becoming the river cop of the Mekong.[48]

Notes

1 Wang Yunfan, 'International judicial cooperation to continue after Naw Kham's execution', *Beijing Times*, quoted in BBC Monitoring Service, 1 March 2013.

2 Andrew R.C. Marshall, 'Special Report: In Mekong', Chinese Murders and Bloody Diplomacy,' Reuters, 27 January 2012.

3 Jeff Howe, *Murder on the Mekong: A Notorious Pirate, a Global Superpower, and a Mystery in the Golden Triangle* (Kindle Single published by Atavist, 2013). An extract is available at https://read.atavist.com/murderonthemekong; and '13 Chinese sailors killed after ships hijacked', Indo Asian News Service, 10 October 2011. Estimates of the Hawngleuk militia's strength vary widely; see, e.g., '12 Chinese murdered in the Mekong River in Chiang Saen District – Murderers executed', *Bangkok Post*, 9 October 2011; Malcolm Moore and David Eimer, 'Mekong massacre trial begins in China', *Telegraph*, 20 September 2012; and Brendan Hong, 'How China Used Drones to Capture a Notorious Burmese Drug Lord', *Daily Beast*, 17 April 2014.

4 'Chinese Foreign Ministry confirms killing of 11 nationals in Thailand', Xinhua, 10 October 2011.

5 *Ibid.*

6 Josh Chin, 'China Vows to Protect Chinese in Libya', *Wall Street Journal*, 25 February 2011.

7 'Chinese Internet users flay sailors' killing in Thailand by drug traffickers', BBC Monitoring Asia Pacific, 10 October 2011.

8 'Thirteen lives lost in Mekong deserve more respect', *Global Times*, 11 October 2011.

9 The Agreement on Commercial Navigation on the Lancang-Mekong River was signed in 2000 and began operation in 2001; see Thein Swe and Paul Chambers, *Cashing In Across the Golden Triangle: Thailand's Northern Border Trade with China, Laos, and Myanmar* (Chiang Mai, Thailand: Mekong Press, 2011), p. 33.

10 'State of the Basin Report 2010', Mekong River Commission, Vientiane, 2010, p. 192, accessed at http://www.mrcmekong.org/assets/Publications/basin-reports/MRC-SOB-report-2010full-report.pdf.

11 Marshall, 'Special Report: In Mekong, Chinese Murders and Bloody Diplomacy'.

12 'China sends patrol vessels to Thailand to bring back stranded ships', Xinhua, 13 October 2011.

13 'Thailand, China to cooperate in probe into Mekong attack', Xinhua, 17 October 2011.

14 'China urges Thailand, Laos, Burma to intensify probe into ship attack', Xinhua, 13 October 2011.

15 'Watchful eye on Mekong River drug trade', *Global Times*, 14 October 2011.

16 'All stranded Chinese sailors return to China after deadly attack', Xinhua, 24 October 2011.

17 Jin Jianyu, 'Mekong countries to boost river security cooperation', *Global Times*, 31 October 2011.

18 'Chinese premier expresses sympathy with Thai flood victims, announces more aid', Xinhua, 29 October 2011.

19 'Securing safety of Mekong', *China Daily*, 13 October 2011.

20 'Watchful eye on Mekong River drug trade', *Global Times*.

21 Zhang Jie 'Meigonghe canan gei Zhongguo de tishi' (What China learned from the cruel Mekong River murders), *Dongfang Zaobao*, (*Oriental Morning Post*), 17 October 2011.

22 'China-Laos-Myanmar-Thailand Meeting on Law Enforcement Cooperation along Mekong River held in Beijing', China Central Television, 31 October 2011, available at http://english.cntv.cn/20111031/112051.shtml; 'China, others to go after "criminals" along the Mekong', Reuters, 31 October 2011; and 'Joint Action To Secure Mekong', Radio Free Asia, 31 October 2011.

23 Zhang Yan 'Suspect stands trial on Mekong killings', *China Daily*, 18 September 2012.

24 *Ibid*.

25 'Manhunt for deadly drug kingpin', *Global Times*, 19 February 2013.

26 Jane Perlez and Bree Feng, 'Beijing Flaunts Cross-Border Clout in Search for Drug Lord', *New York Times*, 4 April 2013.

27 *Ibid*.

28 Howe, *Murder on the Mekong*.

29 Zhang, 'Suspect stands trial on Mekong killings'.

30 'Mekong River suspect pleads guilty', *China Daily*, 23 September 2012.

31 Richard S. Ehrlich, 'Drug lord, gang admit killing Chinese sailors', *Washington Times*, 26 September 2012.

32 Tom Fawthrop, 'Murder on the Mekong', *Diplomat*, 9 December 2011.

33 Jonathan Manthorpe, 'Thai soldiers still awaiting trial for Mekong River murders', *Vancouver Sun*, 17 March 2013; and Jonathan Head, 'Mekong River trial murder mystery', BBC News, 1 September 2012.

34 Jonathan Kaiman, 'China executes four foreign nationals convicted of Mekong river murders', *Guardian*, 1 March 2013.

35 Zhang Yan, 'Mekong suspect denies plotting murders', *China Daily*, 21 September 2012.

36 'Families of Mekong River attack victims compensated', Xinhua, 8 March 2013.

37 Liu Chang, 'Manhunt for deadly drug kingpin', *Global Times*, 9 February 2013.

38 Ian Storey, 'Mekong River Patrols in Full Swing but Challenges Remain', *China Brief* (Jamestown Foundation), vol. 12, no. 4, 21 February 2012.

39 'Zhongguo xunluo meigonghe bianfang buduo huoli peibei bijiao qiangda' (Significant firearm power for Chinese patrols on the Mekong River), Sina.com, 26 April 2013, accessed at http://slide.mil.news.sina.com.cn/slide_8_211_22998.html.

40 'Meigonghe lianhe xunluo yuanman wancheng' (Successful end of joint Mekong River patrol), *Beijing Zhenbao*, 21 March 2015, accessed at http://society.people.com.cn/n/2015/0321/c136657-26727180.html.

41 'Mekong security in focus as China tries drug lord', *China Daily*, 20 September 2012.

42 Storey, 'Mekong River Patrols in Full Swing but Challenges Remain'.

43 Zhang Yan and Guo Anfei, 'Forces from 4 countries save ships from

hijackers', *China Daily*, 20 September 2012.

44 Storey, 'Mekong River Patrols in Full Swing but Challenges Remain'.

45 Zhang, 'Suspect stands trial on Mekong killings'.

46 He Chunzhong, 'Let justice be extended on behalf of the state', *China Youth Daily*, 1 March 2013.

47 He Jingjun, 'Naw Kham's execution to boost protection of overseas citizens', *Beijing News*, 1 March 2013.

48 Ding Gang, 'China can gain prestige as SE Asia's drug cop', *Global Times*, 13 October 2011.

CHAPTER FIVE

International rescue: Beijing's mass evacuation from Libya

Beijing entered a new era in spring 2011 when, as part of a larger evacuation, four Chinese military planes landed in the southern Libyan desert to rescue stranded Chinese workers. It was the time of the Arab Spring, the series of popular uprisings that rapidly toppled long-standing authoritarian governments in Tunisia, Egypt and Libya and sent Syria into a civil war that was still raging in 2015. Those events took the world and China by surprise. Beijing's intention was to continue with business as usual, but the situation didn't permit this.

When unrest and protests spread to President Hosni Mubarak's Egypt in January 2011, official Chinese press coverage had focused on efforts to evacuate the 1,800 Chinese nationals in the country, including 300 Taiwanese in a show of solidarity with China's 'compatriots' on the other side of the Taiwan Strait.[1] This also diverted Chinese press attention and public interest away from sensitive issues such as democracy and social change, which the Arab Spring heralded.

However, Libyan leader Muammar Gadhafi's violent response to the anti-government protests in the eastern city of Benghazi and elsewhere made it impossible for China to completely sit out the Arab Spring. Instead it was compelled to act to protect its interests.

Before 2011, Chinese companies had an expanding footprint in Libya, with investments ranging from oil to construction and telecoms. With these investments followed large cohorts of Chinese labour. Around 36,000 Chinese workers were in Libya when unrest began there in February. They had to be rescued by the Chinese government, state-owned companies and military, working jointly in the largest evacuation mission the People's Republic of China had ever mounted.

China also became at least partially involved in the international response to the Gadhafi regime's brutal crackdown on protesters. Unusually, Beijing was persuaded to vote for United Nations sanctions on Gadhafi in response to alleged human-rights abuses – something that China has normally called an internal matter for a sovereign country. China also acquiesced in the suspension of Libya's membership in the UN Human Rights Council. And rather than using its veto power in the UN Security Council, China abstained on the second UN resolution – Resolution No. 1973 – which authorised the use of force and led to an aerial bombing campaign by NATO that assisted rebels in eventually bringing down the regime.

Although Beijing prefers to deal with established governments, it had to calculate when to establish relations with the Libyan rebels and recognise them as the country's new leaders. The Libyan situation raised the question of which political forces China could rely on when the political chessboard was upset in a third country. Meanwhile, reports that some individuals from Chinese state-owned arms companies were covertly trying to sell weapons to the Gadhafi regime – even as Chinese representatives in the UN voted in favour of an arms embargo – cast a cloud over China's reputation. All of these factors created severe tests for China's principle of non-interference.

Twelve days to pull 35,860 Chinese out of Libya

Few foresaw the events that engulfed the Arab world in 2011, including the Chinese whose presence in the region revolved around commerce and the trade in resources. Initially, Chinese interests didn't seem fundamentally at risk, even though Chinese workers were close to the trouble spots. In Egypt, it was mostly Chinese tourists caught up in the turmoil, and the number of these was relatively low.

In Libya, the Chinese embassy in Tripoli had registered around 6,000 Chinese workers.[2] But the government was in for a surprise, because this was far below the true head count. In reality, around 75 Chinese companies had invested an estimated US$18.8 billion in Libya. These investments were spread across the country, with construction projects in and around Benghazi and Tripoli, oil (CNPC) and hydroelectric (Sinohydro) facilities in the southern desert near Sabha, and several isolated operations in other locations.[3] Adding these workforces together brought the total count to 35,860 Chinese workers (as well as several thousand other foreign staff).

Because China relies on host nations to secure its nationals and commercial interests, it makes diplomatic efforts to maintain close and cordial relations with governments in countries where it has large economic interests, especially in Africa. According to China's special envoy on the Middle East, Wu Sike, 'China's basic principle is to maintain a good relationship with countries of different background and political consciousness, and promote mutually beneficial co-operation with them.'[4] Yet this policy comes under strain when established state power breaks down. That was what happened in Libya. Civil unrest descended into chaos. Chinese companies and workers were under real threat as civil war erupted.

In Ajdabiya, a town in northeastern Libya with around 80,000 inhabitants, Huafeng Construction Company employed more than 1,000 workers on various building sites. Ajdabiya was home to some of the early anti-government protests and was declared a free city on 20 February. During the upheaval, Chinese workers from Huafeng were robbed and forced from their living quarters, essentially making them homeless in a foreign land.[5]

In western Libya, China Communications Construction (CCC) was engaged in building residential homes and infrastructure in the city of Misrata and the town of Bani Walid. CCC had close to 5,000 staff on the ground in Libya and found its project site surrounded by armed gangs. Although the company called local police, they were unable to provide sufficient protection. Instead, the workers organised themselves into vigilante units to protect themselves and 'counter-attacked by throwing stones at the armed gangs', the CCC website reported. 'When the attackers saw the Chinese workers bravely and resolutely standing their ground, the armed gangs dispersed.'[6]

As news spread of Chinese workers being injured in fighting across Libya, it reached the Ministry of Foreign Affairs (MFA) in Beijing, where an anxious consular department started to realise the extent of threat to Chinese nationals. Although the situation was unprecedented, it didn't take long for approval to be given for what Vice Minister of Foreign Affairs Song Tao described as 'the largest and the most complicated overseas evacuation ever conducted by the Chinese government'.[7]

The combined forces of the Chinese state were deployed after President Hu Jintao called on 22 February for 'all-out efforts to bring back Chinese citizens'.[8] Vice premier and Politburo member Zhang Dejiang was placed in charge of the ad hoc task force coordinating the operation,[9] because of his experience as Director of the State Production Safety Commission, responsible for the security of workers inside China.[10] The choice of a Politburo member to head the task force gave it the necessary political clout to issue orders to the military; this would have been impossible had the MFA's consular department been in the driver's seat. Major evacuations need political involvement at the highest level.[11]

What followed in Libya was an unprecedented operation. With Chinese companies and projects spread out across an area three times larger than France, workers were evacuated by land, sea and air. They were taken out through up to eight different countries, with the highest numbers transiting Tunisia, Malta and Greece. A precise breakdown is hard to make, as statistics from the different countries don't precisely add up to the 35,860 figure of total evacuees to which the Chinese government adheres. Several Chinese-language books on the evacuation published with official blessing just rehash news articles from the days of the evacuation without any country-by-country overview of the full evacuation. [12]

On the ground, Chinese government officials and Chinese companies had to find creative ways to get workers out. Many thousands fled through neighbouring Tunisia and a smaller number travelled east into Egypt where the Chinese embassy in Cairo arranged bus transport from the border.[13]

The evacuation task force led by Zhang Dejiang 'decided to immediately deploy chartered civil aircraft, COSCO cargo ships in nearby waters, and Chinese fishing vessels carrying needed living and medical supplies'.[14] The Chinese government also dispatched a team to assist the embassy in Libya, composed of staff from the foreign affairs, commerce and public security ministries, as well as from the State-owned Assets Supervision and Administration Commission (SASAC). The latter is in charge of the largest state-owned enterprises (SOEs) and was thus brought in to coordinate operations with large national players such as the state-run shipping company COSCO.[15] To prove the success of that liaison, a COSCO ship, the MV *Tian*

Fu He, transported 559 workers out of harm's way – a patriotic effort still recorded on the company's website.[16]

The available information on the location of Chinese nationals in the country was scarce, and the Chinese embassy had to request details from major SOEs. The Libyan crisis had exposed the gap between consular registration numbers and the reality on the ground, highlighting the important role played by Chinese firms in the protection of nationals overseas.

Back in China, the national airline, Air China, and its China Eastern Airlines subsidiary made planes available for the evacuation mission. The planes would later fly multiple trips to Crete and Malta, but there were also air transfers to places as far away as Paris and Turkey.

For the first time, Chinese military transport planes took part in the evacuation. This required the stamp of approval from the top military brass in the Central Military Commission. The evacuation task force decided to order IL-76 planes rather than civilian jetliners because of their ability to land on short runways in a potentially chaotic and insecure situation. The four Chinese air-force planes evacuated workers from the remote southern city of Sabha, 600 kilometres from the coast. It remains unconfirmed whether approval was granted by the Libyan authorities, but task-force head Zhang Dejiang declared that the Libyan government hadn't opposed China's decision to send planes.[17]

A number of Sinohydro workers were transported to Khartoum in Sudan and subsequently flown back to China. In total, more than 1,700 Chinese workers were flown into and later out of Sudan. The speed with which Sudan allowed in Chinese military planes was proof of China's long, close-knit relationship with Khartoum, and it raised the possibility of China's working with Sudan as a future African hub for its air force.[18]

However, the main way out of Libya was via sea. The Chinese embassies in Greece and Malta were instructed to hire ships and secure local support. In Greece, the embassy succeeded in renting three ships to extract workers from Libya. The Greek minister for maritime transport later explained that he had contacted shipping companies to secure assistance for China.[19]

In Malta, Chinese Ambassador Zhang Keyuan negotiated exceptions to strict European visa requirements, so that a rented Maltese cruiser could unload Chinese evacuees in Malta and take them directly onto waiting Chinese airplanes without having to complete immigration procedures.[20] Similar arrangements were probably made on the Greek island of Crete where an estimated 15,000 Chinese arrived from Libya. However, other European states would not permit transit through their territory because some Chinese nationals lacked valid passports.[21]

The People's Liberation Army (PLA) was closely involved in decision-making and inter-agency coordination in Beijing, and it executed four distinct missions in Libya: surveillance, deterrence, escort and evacuation (by air). The Chinese navy did not evacuate nationals but the *Xuzhou*, a *Jiangkai*-II class frigate patrolling the Gulf of Aden off the coast of Libya, monitored the security situation and deterred potential threats to the ferries transporting Chinese workers from Libya to Crete and Cyprus.[22]

The *Xuzhou* also provided positive images to beam back home. On Chinese television, viewers could witness happy Chinese evacuees on the *El. Venizelos* waving to the military frigate escorting them to safety.[23] The ship's captain, Wei Jianhua, spoke to the evacuees over the radio exclaiming that 'the strong and prosperous motherland is together with you when you are in hardship'.[24]

The PLA stayed engaged through its defence attachés in embassies across Europe, the Middle East and Northern Africa.[25] Posted at key geographical points across the Libyan border and on ferries, they ensured coordination on the ground to guarantee an orderly evacuation.[26]

These combined efforts bore fruit. On 3 March, the Chinese government could boast that 35,860 Chinese had been evacuated from Libya. The state covered the cost of the operation, according to the Chinese press: US$152 million in total, or US$4,238 (28,000 RMB) per evacuee.[27]

China fine-tunes its non-interference principle

Despite this success, Libya posed a broader foreign-policy conundrum for China. The international community was called upon to act in Libya, and China had to respond to events in the UN Security Council, where it is a permanent veto-wielding member. It also had to figure out its stance towards the Libyan rebels in order to secure influence in post-Gadhafi Libya. Both proved challenges for Chinese foreign policy, in particular for its principle of non-interference.

China voted for UN Security Council Resolution No. 1970 on 26 February 2011, which imposed an arms embargo, travel ban and asset freeze on Gadhafi, his family and certain government officials, and made possible the referral of Gadhafi and other Libyan leaders to the International Criminal Court for crimes against humanity. Going far beyond China's usual foreign-policy inclinations, the resolution deplored 'the gross and systematic violation of human rights, including the repression of peaceful demonstrators' in Libya. On the human-rights front, China went along with an unprecedented suspension of Libya from the Human Rights Council, decided by consensus in the UN General Assembly on 1 March. The Chinese representative, Zhang Dan, only meekly upheld the established

Chinese line by stressing that this action should not set a precedent.[28]

What explains China's take on Libya, given its track record of shielding authoritarian regimes such as Myanmar, Zimbabwe and North Korea in the UN? Chinese UN representative Li Baodong emphasised Beijing's concern about the situation in Libya and also specifically stressed that 'the safety and interest of the foreign nationals in Libya must be assured'. Li also said that special circumstances in Libya had persuaded China to vote in favour of the resolution. These special circumstances included demands from the African Union and the Arab League for an international response, as well as China's own strained relations with Gadhafi.[29]

Customarily, China would rely on a host government to protect Chinese nationals in a time of conflict. The fact that the Gadhafi regime wasn't able to shield Chinese workers in the chaotic days of revolution prompted Beijing to act to safeguard its citizens. Resolution 1970 included a specific provision urging the Libyan government to 'ensure the safety of all foreign nationals and their assets'. The regime's obvious inability to guarantee stability on its own soil, as it battled for survival in a growing civil war, also meant that China was less willing to give Libya any form of protective cover in the UN.

China abstained on the later UN Security Council resolution, No. 1973, which authorised the international community 'to take all necessary measures ... to protect civilians and civilian populated areas under threat of attack in the Libyan Arab Jamahiriya, including Benghazi' and which authorised no-fly zones enforced by NATO and its allies. However, even this abstention – as opposed to a veto – marked a departure from China's usual position. In 1999, China and Russia had blocked a similar resolution over Kosovo.

However, Beijing's position on Libya was not unequivocal. Later witnessing the military actions by NATO and partners in Libya, China made efforts to portray this abstention to its people as a 'no' vote, declaring that military action was likely to cause more civilian casualties. The MFA was reportedly criticised by the Chinese military for not foreseeing the Western military action that the imposition of a no-fly zone permitted.

By late April, President Hu Jintao warned visiting French President Nicolas Sarkozy that, 'If the military action brings disaster to innocent civilians, resulting in an even greater humanitarian crisis, then that is contrary to the original intention of the Security Council resolution.'[30] Later, in the same vein, China declared that the NATO operation had overstepped the mandate given to it by the UN, by facilitating regime change in Libya. This influenced Beijing's subsequent resistance to UN action in Syria when that country also descended into civil war.

Dealing with the Libyan rebels

In September 2011, an additional Chinese foreign-policy dilemma turned up in a pile of rubbish in the suburbs of Tripoli. In the garbage was a memo describing exploratory arms-sale negotiations between Libya and China. The memo detailed a trip by Gadhafi officials to Beijing in mid-July, in which they met with several Chinese state-owned arms manufacturers, including China North Industries Corporation (Norinco), the China National Precision Machinery Import and Export Corporation (CPMIC), and China XinXing Import and Export Corporation. These companies offered to sell weapons ranging from truck-mounted rocket launchers to fuel-air explosive missiles, anti-tank missiles and QW-18 surface-to-air missiles. The weapons were supposed to be shipped through Algeria, depending on further talks and consent from Algiers.[31]

Had the arms been delivered, China and the consortium of arms-trade companies would have been in contravention of the UN arms embargo on Libya. When the news of the negotiations emerged, Beijing initially declined to comment on the issue in line with the 'laying low' tenet of Chinese foreign policy. Technically no Chinese export-control laws were violated, as no regulations prevent individuals from informally discussing possible arms sales with foreign entities. The Chinese companies would only have had to apply for authorisation to start formal negotiations. Still, the Norinco employee concerned was subsequently removed from his post, the company has said, for acting against Chinese foreign-policy interests.[32]

International and Libyan disapproval compelled China to provide an account of events. Four days after the disclosure, Chinese MFA spokeswoman Jiang Yu declared that Chinese companies had not provided military equipment to Libya, directly or indirectly, since the adoption of UN Security Council Resolution No. 1970. She added that, 'China exercises strict management over all military exports.'[33]

Yet in a sense the damage was already done, because Libya's new powers-to-be in the National Transition Council (NTC) now viewed China with suspicion. Some in Libya suggested there was no place in the post-war reconstruction process for nations that had not backed military support to the rebels.[34] Abdeljalil Mayuf, spokesman for the Arabian Gulf Oil Company (Agoco), said that Beijing had 'gambled on the wrong horse' and expected Chinese contracts to be cancelled. Rebel fighters publicly designated China an 'unfriendly' country.[35]

China had kept up relations with the government of Gadhafi, but had hedged its bets by establishing contacts with the NTC as early as May 2011 through its embassies in Cairo and Qatar. China also quietly participated in the 'Friends of Libya' summit, hosted in Paris by French President Nicolas Sarkozy on 1 September.

China was the only major holdout after Russia recognised the NTC in early September – the only permanent Security Council member still with official ties to the Gadhafi regime. Around the same time the news surfaced about China's alleged arms deals with Gadhafi. Finally, on 12 September, Beijing recognised the NTC as the legitimate government of Libya. 'China respects the choice of the Libyan people,' said MFA spokesman Ma Zhaoxu in a statement.[36]

According to analysis published by China expert Yun Sun, the Chinese conclusion was that its initial 'support' for UNSCR No. 1973 had been in vain.[37] It decided that it had gained nothing with the new powers in Tripoli or with the West, which helps explain China's much more recalcitrant attitude during subsequent UN debates on Syria. Another article argues that China was 'taught a lesson', learning that 'an attractive economic partner' isn't the same as an 'attractive ally'.[38]

One of the lessons of Libya for China was to diversify its political contacts. This was something Chinese diplomacy did skillfully in Pakistan, for example, but a practice that still remains the exception.

However, examining the economic data in 2014, it looked as if any Chinese setbacks in Libya were temporary. Economic logic seemed to have prevailed, and when the then-Libyan Foreign Minister Ben Ashour Khayil travelled to China in mid-2012 he expressed appreciation for China's 'fair and responsible' position and invited China to join in Libya's post-war reconstruction.[39] A 2013 report to the US Congress concluded that, despite a decline in 2011, trade between China and Libya rebounded in 2012 and the first six months of 2013 (especially Chinese exports to Libya).[40]

Beijing's new, keener perception of risk

After the unprecedented evacuation from Libya, Chinese grand strategist Yan Xuetong claimed that China's policy in this instance was 'clearly a break' from the practice of keeping a low profile.[41] The Arab Spring and Libya's violent revolution had several consequences for Chinese foreign policy. It showed the limits of economic diplomacy without wider engagement. It highlighted the risk management necessary in unstable countries and the foreign-policy implications of having workers in such countries – including the need to rescue them and to appropriately position itself in the UN and international system. After Libya, Middle East envoy Wu Sike announced that China would maintain economic ties with 'all the countries' in the region. 'But we will definitely also improve our risk assessment and prevention mechanisms,' he added.[42]

The Libyan crisis compelled China to carry out its largest evacuation mission, combining all of its available resources. It emerged from the experience with a new commitment, its own uniquely Chinese version of a 'responsibility to protect' its own citizens and workers abroad. This has consequences for future crises, in line with Hu Jintao's command to 'spare no efforts to ensure the safety of life and properties of Chinese citizens' in Libya. The involvement of the military also set a precedent, although the PLA played a minor role, especially if one were to compare it, say, with the American deployment of more than 5,000 marines and sailors to evacuate 15,000 US nationals from Lebanon in 2006.[43]

The institutionalisation of consular protection and the capacity-building described in Chapter Two accelerated after Libya. If Afghanistan and Pakistan woke China to the importance of protecting its national interests overseas, Libya gave Beijing a taste of the scale of the task and the importance of the resources it might have to commit in future. However, China may have created a rod for its own back with the success of its Libyan evacuation, for it has raised expectations among Chinese citizens and companies regarding their government's ability to act in future cases. Clearly, this might entail additional unwanted involvement abroad if future rescues fail to run as smoothly as in Libya.

After the no-fly zone over Libya was enacted by UNSCR No. 1973, the Chinese press portrayed events in Libya as a foreign military intervention and stopped mentioning China's voting record on UN resolutions. Beijing wished to convey the message to the Chinese public that foreign military intervention worsens instability and chaos. There was no desire to talk publicly of democratic transition and 'people power', or suggest that rebellion could be justified. This domestic messaging was at odds with China's diplomatic efforts in securing a place in Libya's future and reconstruction.[44]

By the time Syria had descended into full-blown civil war in June 2011, China's opposition to Western-led sanctions and intervention had hardened. It was less willing to endorse UN actions and it rejected several draft UNSC resolutions on Syria, which it thought covered internal matters for the Syrian government. What China did take away from Libya was a pragmatic approach towards speaking with rebels. Therefore, early on in the Syrian conflict Beijing reached out to the opposition, so as not to be wrong-footed should they gain the advantage on the battlefield.

Although China eventually returned in Syria to a policy of non-interference, the momentous events in Libya had taught Beijing how to better deal with the burdens of an increasing economic and human presence overseas. While China had demonstrated, both domestically and abroad, the efficiency of its logistics, questions as to the 'costs of Libya' still linger. Chinese companies did not specify their losses during the Libyan uprising, but the Ministry of Commerce has officially demanded compensation from Libya, particularly for housing projects, worth more than US$10bn which were badly damaged during the war.[45] The evacuation safeguarded Chinese nationals, but did not solve the larger question of the protection of wider Chinese interests in the Middle East.

Libya stretched the boundaries of China's policy of non-interference, but its evacuation from the country appeared to be a last resort – getting out rather than getting involved, even if that meant paying an exit price.

Notes

[1] 'Backgrounder: China's major overseas evacuations in recent years', Xinhua, 20 March 2015.

[2] Chinese official, Author interview, Beijing, January 2013.

[3] 'Zhanhuo xia de zhongguo zichan' (Chinese assets in the war), *Jinri Gongcheng Jiqi (Today's engineering and mechanics)*, vol. 115, September 2011, pp. 72–6.

[4] Ng Tze-wei, 'China on track in Mid-East but US losing its way, envoy says', *South China Morning Post*, 11 March 2011.

[5] 'China urges Libya to ensure nationals' safety: envoy', Xinhua, 22 February 2011.

[6] Toh Han Shih, '10.7b yuan worth of projects at risk in Libya, 2 Chinese companies say', *South China Morning Post*, 4 March 2011.

[7] '35,860 Chinese nationals in Libya evacuated: FM', *People's Daily*, 3 March 2011.

[8] 'All-Out Efforts To Bring Back Chinese Citizens in Libya', Xinhua, 23 February 2011.

[9] 'Libiya cheqiao quan jilu: 500 yugong renban tebia ban huigguo zhenming' (The full story of the Libyan evacuation: more than 500 workers home), *Zhongguo Xinwen Zhoukan (China Newsweek)*, 10 March 2011, accessed at http://news.sina.com.cn/c/sd/2011-03-10/145222088651.shtml.

[10] Chinese diplomat, Author interview, Beijing, February 2012.

[11] The task-force model proved successful and could be replicated in future, although the establishment of a National Security Commission at the Third Plenum of the 18th Central Committee in November 2013 has given China a new means of coordinating foreign and security policy.

[12] Such books include Jianming He, *Guo Jia (The Nation)* (Beijing: The Writers Publishing House, 2012); and *National Action: The Libya Evacuation* (Beijing: The People's Daily Press, 2011).

[13] MFA figures say 100 coaches were rented; see Hao Yalin and Liu Chang, 'Foreign Ministry Spokesman: Chinese Side To Do Everything Possible To Do Good

Job of Evacuating Personnel From Libya', Xinhua, 24 February 2011.

14 MFA statement quoted in 'China sends plane, ships for Libya evacuation', Agence France-Presse, 23 February 2011.

15 Hao and Liu, 'Foreign Ministry Spokesman: Chinese Side To Do Everything Possible To Do Good Job of Evacuating Personnel From Libya'.

16 See 'About COSCO, History', COSCO, accessed at http://en.cosco.com/col/col770/index.html.

17 Mathieu Duchâtel, Oliver Bräuner and Zhou Hang, 'China's Globalizing Interests, the slow shift away from non-interference', SIPRI Policy Paper No. 41, June 2014, p. 49.

18 See similar considerations in Gabe Collins and Andrew S. Erickson, 'Implications of China's Military Evacuation of Citizens from Libya', China Brief (Jamestown Foundation), vol. 11, no. 4, 10 March 2011.

19 'China Strives To Evacuate Nationals From Libya, Gets Aid From Foreign Governments', Xinhua, 26 February 2011.

20 'The full story of the Libyan evacuation', China Newsweek.

21 EU official, Author interview, Brussels, December 2012.

22 Li Faxin, The Chinese Navy's Maritime Escort Operations (Beijing: China Intercontinental Press, 2013), pp. 54–8.

23 Footage of Chinese evacuees in front of the Greek ship El. Venizelos, accessed at 6'27" at http://v.youku.com/v_show/id_XMzIxNDAxMDU2.html.

24 'Meimei: Libiya dongtang jiance zhongguo de zhongdong liyi' (American Press: Libya's Turmoil is Testing China's Interest in Middle East), 2 March 2011, accessed at http://national.dwnews.com/big5/news/2011-03-02/57454151.html.

25 The embassies involved were in Greece, Tunisia, Algeria, Egypt, Sudan, Yemen, Kuwait, Turkey, Italy, Slovakia, Denmark, Finland and Sweden.

26 Gao Jiquan, 'Zhongguo wuguan zhandi biji: zhuwai wuguan yanzhong de libiya de cheli xingdong' (Battle memories of Chinese Defense Attachés: the great Libyan evacuation operation seen by DA), Jiefangjunbao (PLA Daily), 7 March 2011. An abstract can be accessed online at http://218.22.190.134/QK/80410B/201105/37895374.html.

27 Shaio H. Zerba, 'China's Libya Evacuation Operation: a new diplomatic imperative – overseas citizens protection', Journal of Contemporary China, vol. 23, no. 90, pp. 1,093–102.

28 'General Assembly suspends Libya from Human Rights Council', coverage of the 76th meeting of the 65th United Nations General Assembly, 1 March 2011, accessed at http://www.un.org/News/Press/docs/2011/ga11050.doc.htm.

29 'In swift, decisive action, Security Council imposes tough measures on Libyan regime, adopting Resolution 1970 in wake of crackdown on protesters', coverage of the 6,491st UN Security Council meeting, 26 February 2011, accessed at http://www.un.org/News/Press/docs/2011/sc10187.doc.htm.

30 'China to Support Infrastructure Development in Arab States', Xinhua, 22 September 2011.

31 Graeme Smith, 'China offered Gadhafi huge stockpiles of arms: Libyan memos', *Globe and Mail*, 2 September 2011.

32 Mark Bromley, Mathieu Duchâtel and Paul Holtom, *China's Exports of Small Arms and Light Weapons*, SIPRI Policy Paper No. 38, October 2013, p. 12.

33 Michael Wines, 'Beijing Says Qaddafi Officials Sought Chinese Arms Supplies', *New York Times*, 5 September 2011.

34 Andrew Higgins, 'Libya policy a balancing act for China as Moammar Gaddafi's rule collapses', *Washington Post*, 27 August 2011.

35 Chris Stephen, Caroline Alexander and Ladane Nasseri, 'China Vows to Toughen Control After Report of Libya Arm Sales', Bloomberg, 6 September 2011.

36 'China recognizes Libya's NTC as ruling authority, representative of people', Xinhua, 12 September 2011.

37 Yun Sun, 'Syria: What China Has Learned From its Libya Experience', *Asia Pacific Bulletin*, no. 152, February 2012.

38 Stephanie Erian, 'China at the Libyan Endgame', *Policy* (Australia), vol. 28, no. 1, Autumn 2012; and Yun, 'Syria: What China Has Learned From its Libya Experience'. A similar analysis is found in 'Libya

reveals disconnects in China's foreign policy', Oxford Analytica Daily Brief, 6 October 2011.

39 MFA, 'Vice President Xi Jinping Meets with Libyan Foreign Minister', 11 June 2012, accessed at http://www.fmprc.gov.cn/mfa_eng/wjb_663304/zzjg_663340/xybfs_663590/gjlb_663594/2848_663686/2850_663690/t941359.shtml.

40 'China and the world', Annual Report to Congress 2013, U.S.–CHINA Economic and Security Review Commission, p. 310, accessed at http://www.uscc.gov/Annual_Reports/2013-annual-report-congress.

41 Yan Xuetong, 'How assertive should a great power be?', *International Herald Tribune*, 31 March 2011.

42 Ng, 'China on track in Mid-East but US losing its way, envoy says'.

43 Shaio, 'China's Libya Evacuation Operation: a new diplomatic imperative – overseas citizens protection', pp. 1,101–02.

44 See further elaboration on this in Jonas Parello-Plesner and Raffaello Pantucci, 'China's Janus-faced response to the Arab revolutions', European Council on Foreign Relations (ECFR) Policy Memo, May 2011.

45 'China asks Libya to compensate for companies' losses', Xinhua, 7 March 2012.

CHAPTER SIX

China in deep in the oil-rich Sudans

Of all the countries with a significant Chinese economic and human presence, the Sudans have been the biggest test of Beijing's principle of non-interference. Although China has made great efforts to stick purely to business, the region's turbulent history has gradually pulled it in diplomatically and politically. Sudan was an early target of China's 'going-out' policy; here state-owned oil company China National Petroleum Corporation (CNPC) made its first large international investment in the mid-1990s after sanctions on Khartoum had forced Western companies to leave. South Sudan, which gained independence from the north in July 2011, has been one of the first overseas locations where China has stationed combat troops, albeit as part of a United Nations mission.[1]

Strategically important to Beijing as host to various Chinese oil and other businesses,[2] Sudan has always harboured multiple risks for Chinese firms. Alongside Pakistan, this is a place where Chinese interests and nationals have been targeted simply for being Chinese. As a result, China's policy in Sudan has shifted. In 2004–06, Beijing shied away from taking a stance on events in Sudan's Darfur region, which Western campaigners described as ethnic cleansing of black African tribes by 'Janjaweed' militias supported by the Arab-dominated government in Khartoum. Since 2011, however, China has been deeply engaged in shuttle diplomacy to try to persuade warring parties in the north and south back to the negotiating table and to encourage them to respect pipeline agreements and keep the oil flowing – all the way to China.

When a split in the new government in South Sudan in December 2013 swiftly descended into full-scale civil war, Chinese companies were forced to evacuate several hundred Chinese workers caught in the turmoil, as they had done in Libya. In May 2014 in the UN Security Council, China further broke new ground when in the negotiations over the extension of the peacekeeping mandate of the United Nations Mission in South Sudan (UNMISS), China secured the inclusion of the protection of oil workers, thus securing its own interests in volatile South Sudan.

An African oil rush

Oil was China's original incentive to engage in Sudan. In 2010, the unified Sudan was the second-largest oil producer in Africa outside OPEC, producing 490,000 barrels per day (bpd)[3] – of which the lion's share went to China.[4] Conflict since the two countries' separation saw Sudan and South Sudan's combined output slip to 115,000 bpd in 2012, before recovering to 250,000 bpd in 2013. In 2014, South Sudan was estimated to be sitting on 3.5 billion barrels of proven oil reserves, while Sudan had 1.5bn.[5]

China entered the Sudanese market in September 1995 when CNPC, one of its top three state-owned oil companies, signed an agreement with Khartoum to develop Block 6 in the Muglad Rift Basin. US oil major Chevron first found oil in the Muglad Basin, some 700 kilometres south of Khartoum, in the late 1970s. However, in the 1990s Western oil countries left Sudanese exploration after Washington designated Khartoum a state sponsor of terrorism.[6] China had become a net importer of oil in 1993 and state oil majors were urged to find new external energy supplies through international expansion. The idea of investing in Sudan also dovetailed with CNPC's corporate plan for the diversification of international opportunities. In November 1996, outbidding other oil companies, CNPC – then headed by Zhou Yongkang – won the contract to develop Blocks 1/2/4 in the Muglad Basin.

China's oil engagement in Sudan expanded swiftly. By 1998, when CNPC and its partners in the Greater Nile Petroleum Operating Company (GNPOC) had already established a 10 million-ton production capacity at Blocks 1/2/4, CNPC won the contract to build a 1,500km oil-export pipeline from the Muglad oil field to the coast at Port Sudan.[7] In August 1999, the first tanker load of 600,000 barrels of Sudanese oil departed, and Sudan was soon an important energy supplier to China. In 2002, it provided close to 10% of China's oil imports. Since then the percentage has dwindled due to China's energy diversification and due to Sudan's plummeting production. In 2010, it produced close to 500,000 barrels per day of which some 80% went to China.[8] In China's overall oil imports that year, Sudan ranked only second in Africa, after OPEC member Angola.

At the time of the initial investments, neither CNPC nor the Chinese government gave much consideration to the local risk factors in their oil investments in Sudan. However, South Sudanese independence in 2011 fundamentally changed the situation. Most of the region's oil fields ended up in South Sudan, several of them in disputed border regions. And while South Sudan gained the lion's share of oil reserves, its land-locked geography meant that its exports were entirely reliant on the pipeline, built with Chinese assistance, travelling across

Sudan to Port Sudan, where oil tankers docked. The potential for dispute was obvious and it swiftly resulted in bitter disagreement. Gradually, CNPC and the Chinese government have had to intervene to try to secure – so far unsuccessfully – an uninterrupted flow of oil.

Beijing under fire over Darfur

In fact, several regions of Sudan have seen prolonged conflict. Civil war raged in the south from 1983 until 2005. In the western region of Darfur, rebels from the Sudan Liberation Movement (SLM) and the Justice and Equality Movement (JEM) started targeting the government in 2003, accusing Khartoum of backing Janjaweed militias attacking African villages. The SLM and JEM claimed this was an attempt to drive them from their land; some Western NGOs branded it full-blown genocide. Although Khartoum denied links to the Janjaweed, in 2008 the International Criminal Court issued an arrest warrant for Sudan's President Omar al-Bashir on charges of war crimes, crimes against humanity and genocide.[9] An estimated 300,000 or more have died in the violence in Darfur and up to 3m have been internally displaced. However, as the conflicts in both Darfur and the south unfolded, the booming relationship between China and Sudan expanded into other areas besides energy, including weapons and telecommunications. From early on, Beijing maintained that its political relationship with the regime in Khartoum was based on respect for non-interference in a country's internal affairs and on the goal of securing business interests. Thus, in 2005, China's deputy foreign minister declared: 'Business is business. We try to separate politics... the internal situation in Sudan is an internal affair.'[10]

To outside observers, however, China appeared to be engaged in 'dictator diplomacy', shielding Khartoum from a barrage of international criticism by blocking or diluting efforts to provide UN humanitarian aid and international conflict resolution in Darfur. In September 2004, when the United States drafted a UN Security Council resolution to impose oil sanctions on Sudan for its failure to protect its own citizens in Darfur, China threatened to use its veto.[11] In April 2006, China abstained on another UN Security Council resolution successfully installing targeted sanctions on four Sudanese officials.[12]

Very soon afterwards, China's stance began to shift because international pressure about Darfur was beginning to threaten its own reputation. For example, in April 2006 an international civil-society campaign began targeting the forthcoming Olympic Games in Beijing in an attempt to persuade China to compel Khartoum to bring peace to Darfur.[13] With the 2008 Summer Games branded by campaigners as the 'genocide Olympics', China was concerned that one of its most prestigious projects would be tarnished, possibly even boycotted.

In any case, China appeared to respond to campaigners' calls for a new UN-led peacekeeping mission to replace a small African Union (AU) force in Darfur, by stepping up the pressure on Khartoum to accept international peacekeepers. In November 2006 at a high-level meeting in Ethiopia, China's representative to the AU first suggested a hybrid AU–UN mission to accommodate Sudan's desire for an 'African' peace operation.[14] On a visit to Khartoum in February 2007, President Hu Jintao pointedly told Sudan's President Bashir to make room for an AU–UN presence in Darfur.[15]

On 10 May 2007, China appointed a special diplomatic envoy, Liu Guijin, to focus on the Darfur crisis. The move came just days after 108 US legislators wrote to President Hu urging him to change policy towards Sudan or face disaster for the Beijing Olympics.[16] At the same time, China was also being accused of supplying arms to Sudan for use in Darfur, in contravention of a UN arms embargo. When the new African

Union/United Nations Hybrid operation in Darfur (UNAMID) was created by the UN Security Council at the end of July 2007, China sought to deflect any further criticism by contributing engineering troops. All of these were signs of a slightly more active Chinese approach towards Sudan.

There had been constant danger for Chinese workers in the war-torn country. Already in 2004, two Chinese oil workers had been killed in Sudan, and two others had been kidnapped but escaped. However, no rebel group took responsibility for this attack nor was there anything to suggest it was targeted at Chinese interests.[17]

The situation changed in 2007 when Beijing's close links with Khartoum brought Chinese interests into the sights of the Darfuri rebel group JEM. In October 2007, JEM stormed the GNPOC-run Diffra oil field in neighbouring South Kordofan state, killing Sudanese soldiers and kidnapping five oil workers.[18] Although none of the hostages was Chinese, the kidnapping came with a clear warning to China that its companies should leave the country and that it should stop supporting the Sudanese government.[19] JEM's chief negotiator, Ahmed Tugud, explained that all of the weapons taken from soldiers during the attack were Chinese. 'The Sudan government is using the oil money it gets from China to buy weapons to kill our people,' he declared.[20] The Chinese Ministry of Foreign Affairs (MFA) made no comment other than to say that Chinese oil workers were safe and the Sudanese government should assure their safety.[21]

In 2008, matters worsened at Diffra when JEM killed five of nine Chinese workers it had kidnapped. Chinese officials involved in the negotiations to try to secure the hostages' safe release have told us that Beijing asked the International Committee of the Red Cross to help mediate, but also engaged directly with rebel leaders. Official Chinese policy is not to pay ransoms, as this is seen as encouraging additional hostage-taking. However, there apparently exists a pragmatic, case-by-case approach. In this case, according to a former Chinese diplomat involved in the transaction, there appeared to be an indirect ransom in the form of promises of local development projects or humanitarian aid benefiting JEM.[22]

Adjusting to South Sudanese independence

In the south a civil war had been raging since the 1980s between Khartoum and rebels from the southern Sudan People's Liberation Movement (SPLM). China was a marginal player during the negotiations that led to the signing in 2005 of the Comprehensive Peace Agreement between the two parties. Beijing's insistence on non-interference, while prioritising relationships and arms sales directly with Khartoum, didn't give it much sway with the SPLM leaders.

China only seemed to realise what challenges lay ahead after a visit to Beijing in 2007 by Sudan's then-vice-president and head of the southern regional government, Salva Kiir. Kiir reportedly flashed a map of the location of major oil fields and explained the possibility of the south's secession. That opened Chinese eyes to the prospect of a new southern state hosting most of CNPC's oil fields.[23]

As a result, Beijing began to hedge its bets by reaching out to the south. It opened a consulate in Juba in 2008, providing new direct lines of contact, and it also sought assurances that its oil investments would be safe in a future South Sudan. A Communist Party delegation visited Juba in 2010 to check on this.[24] In 2011, Vice Foreign Minister Zhang Zhijun and CNPC officials were dispatched to Juba to jointly reiterate Chinese concerns about the security of the country's oil investments.[25]

Because of the Taiwan issue, China does not normally countenance secession. However, it took a pragmatic line in the

run-up to the 2009 referendum on South Sudanese independence, talking of the need for a peaceful, credible vote and of
respect for the choice of the Sudanese people.[26] It even provided
US$500,000 in assistance for the South Sudanese Referendum
Commission and dispatched an observation team.[27] Two years
later, in July 2011, President Hu sent a trusted confidant to attend
the celebration of South Sudan's independence, and immediately upgraded the Chinese consulate in Juba to an embassy.
China was also quick to move into infrastructure development
in the new nation, building the Legislative Assembly. It also
provided assistance in education and health.[28]

Yet none of these moves insulated China from future difficulties for its oil industry. Negotiations between Sudan and
South Sudan on how to divide oil revenues (and demarcate
their border) had serious repercussions. Landlocked South
Sudan's dependence on the export pipeline passing through
Sudan prompted questions of transit fees. Obtaining the best
deal was vital for both sides. Sudan had lost three-quarters of
its oil industry in the south's secession; South Sudan began life
as one of the world's poorest countries, reliant on oil for 98% of
its government revenues.

In an attempt to make up for lost oil earnings, Sudan
requested transit fees of US$32 per barrel; South Sudan coun-
tered with an offer of US$1 per barrel. In December 2011, Sudan
began confiscating South Sudanese oil in 'payment' for alleged
transit-fee arrears. South Sudan accused Khartoum of theft
and shut down oil production in January 2012.[29] Its main aim
in doing this was to place pressure on Khartoum, but it also
wanted to encourage Beijing, the main recipient of the oil, to
use its leverage on Khartoum to accept concessions in renewed
negotiations.

From a Chinese perspective, the situation deteriorated in
February 2012 when Liu Yingcai, the Chinese head of Petrodar

– the other oil consortium in South Sudan in which CNPC has a stake – was expelled by Juba. Liu was accused of a lack of cooperation in implementing the oil-production shutdown and in colluding with Sudanese authorities in loading South Sudanese oil onto tankers at Port Sudan.[30] Petrodar was also accused by Juba of secretly producing more oil than it had declared.

Soon afterwards, China offered to mediate in the transit-fees dispute, and during nearly 15 months of on/off negotiations, its special envoy, Zhong Jianhua, shuttled back and forth between the parties to get them to talk.[31] Eventually, in March 2013, the two countries came to an agreement, and oil production resumed the next month. Yet there would be only a short-lived period of peace before a split in the ruling party in South Sudan in December 2013 plunged the young country into a new civil war.

Chinese lives held to ransom

In January 2012 – as Sudan and South Sudan remained locked in dispute over oil transit fees – 29 Chinese road workers employed by a subsidiary of Sinohydro were kidnapped in the Sudanese province of South Kordofan. The perpetrators were rebels from the SPLM–North (SPLM–N), members of the southern secessionist movement who remained in Sudan continuing the fight against Khartoum.

China responded swiftly to the mass kidnapping. In Beijing, Vice-Foreign Minister Xie Hangsheng summoned the Sudanese embassy to demand the protection of Chinese nationals. Additionally, a joint team from the ministries of foreign affairs, commerce, public security and the State-owned Assets Supervision and Administration Commission (SASAC) was dispatched to Sudan. China prefers to let local authorities take the lead, but through this step also demonstrated its improved institutional capacity to safeguard its nationals. Meanwhile, the Chinese ambassador to Ethiopia met SPLM–N rebel leader Malik Agar, who demanded Chinese assistance in persuading Khartoum to let much-needed humanitarian aid into the South Kordofan conflict zone.[32]

As had happened when Chinese lives were endangered or lost in Libya (see Chapter Five) and on the Mekong River (see Chapter Four), the kidnappings provoked hundreds of thousands of comments in the Chinese blogosphere,[33] with Chinese netizens lamenting Beijing's inability to protect its own workers or act like other great powers and dispatch special forces. The nationalist *Global Times* newspaper noted wryly that China was still not 'powerful enough' to protect its interests in Africa.[34]

After an intense ten days of conflicting news reports, the Chinese workers were released through the auspices of the International Committee of the Red Cross. The Chinese MFA issued a statement noting, in language which has become the new reference position, that: 'The Sudanese foreign ministry affirms to the government and people of China that Sudan's government seeks to protect Chinese investments and workers involved in it.'[35] It seems likely that the Chinese employed similar tactics as in 2008 where the 'ransom' consisted in Chinese promises of local development. This is especially likely, given that one of the SPLM–N's initial demands was for humanitarian access and supplies.

Rescuing Chinese workers from a new civil war

In December 2013, civil war erupted as South Sudanese President Salva Kiir accused his former vice-president, Riek Machar, of plotting a coup. What began as a fight at an army barracks in Juba on 15 December between troops loyal to each man rapidly split the country down ethnic lines, pitting Kiir's majority Dinka community against Machar's Nuer minority. The fighting caused oil production to plummet and severely affected oil-producing states, such as Unity and Upper Nile. Again, Chinese interests and workers were caught in the middle.

The Chinese embassy in Juba estimated that 2,300 Chinese nationals were present in South Sudan before the outbreak of hostilities. On 19 December, violence spread to the country's oil fields when 14 local workers were killed at a Sudd Petroleum Operating Company (SPOC) facility in the Muglad Basin. Although only Malaysian, Indian and South Sudanese companies have stakes in SPOC, CNPC initiated the evacuation of its own personnel.[36]

The Chinese embassy in Juba triggered the emergency-response mechanism, a new system run by the Chinese MFA to coordinate threats and evacuations following after the successful joint intergovernmental cooperation in Libya.[37] Immediately, travel warnings were sent out.[38] There were particular difficulties in Unity state where fighting forced 200 oil workers from unnamed companies to seek refuge in a nearby UN camp.[39] Taking charge of its own operations, CNPC evacuated more than 400 oil workers in eight chartered planes, airlifting them to Khartoum on 25 December.[40] By then, according to the Chinese embassy, half of the estimated 2,300 nationals in South Sudan had been evacuated. Half of those remaining were in the northern oil fields, it said, with another 570 in Juba.[41]

The Chinese embassy in Khartoum liaised with Sudanese contacts to ensure the safe transit, by land and air, of evacuees, since few of the Chinese workers held Sudanese visas.[42] Reportedly, Chinese UN peacekeepers also assisted in rescue and evacuation operations, helping at least 15 Chinese nationals get away to safety. The peacekeepers also seemed to have apprised CNPC of local security assessments in Upper Nile state.[43]

Even after the evacuation of Chinese nationals, the civil war in South Sudan continued to impact upon Chinese interests.

Matters might have been worse if CNPC had been based in Unity state where Riek Machar's supporters initially gained a stronghold. However, even in Upper Nile state, where CNPC has large stakes, the effects have been deleterious. Upper Nile produces 80% of South Sudan's oil and its fields have been kept running by essential workers, with a plane on standby to evacuate them at the last minute. Despite this, the state's oil production plummeted by one-third to 160,000 barrels per day.[44]

China dons blue helmets out of national self-interest

For evidence of how invested – in all senses of the word – China is in South Sudan, one only need consider the 'delight and relief' expressed by the Chinese ambassador to Ethiopia, Xie Xiaoyan, 'on behalf of the Chinese people' when a first ceasefire was announced at the end of January 2014 after negotiations in Addis Ababa.[45] Such a public display of emotion is unusual for normally reserved Chinese diplomats.

Unfortunately, the ink was barely dry on the ceasefire agreement before the first violations occurred. After the second ceasefire in May 2014, China committed US$3m to the Intergovernmental Authority on Development (IGAD), the East African bloc negotiating and monitoring peace in South Sudan. The Chinese grant included US$1m to the IGAD mechanism to monitor the implementation of the ceasefire.[46] As the Chinese ambassador to Juba, Ma Qiang, stated clearly: 'We have huge interests in South Sudan, so we have to make a greater effort to persuade the two sides to stop fighting and agree to a ceasefire.' Ambassador Ma himself directly intervened, securing South Sudanese government permission for the UN to relocate a camp, mostly housing displaced Nuer, in danger of flooding with the onset of the rainy season. The government's initial reluctance to relocate the camp was overcome by CNPC's offer to pay nearly US$2m to build the new camp.[47]

Nevertheless, striking the correct balance proved difficult. SPLM–IO rebels viewed the fact that Chinese state-owned arms dealer Norinco was planning to supply large quantities of weapons to the South Sudanese government as compromising China's role as a mediator. Although only a small number of arms were delivered before the Chinese government halted further dispatches, SPLM-IO spokesman Mabior Garang de Mabior made a jibe at China's apparent ability to simultaneously support the war effort and peace talks.[48] However, China also demonstrated a new-found fleet-footedness in times of governmental instability, by receiving a delegation of SPLM-IO rebels who flew to Beijing in September 2014 to ask it not to sell weapons to Juba.[49] In January 2015, China actively encouraged and attended an IGAD-led peace conference in the Sudanese capital, Khartoum, bringing together the warring parties from South Sudan. Chinese Foreign Minister Wang Yi described China as an 'active promoter' of peace, and defended China's obvious interest in seeing a ceasefire as being more than just about oil.[50]

The same Chinese activism was evident when the mandate of the 14,000-strong UNMISS peacekeeping force was extended and revised in May 2014. UN Security Council Resolution 2155 authorised UNMISS to use 'all necessary means' to protect civilians, monitor and investigate human rights, create the conditions for delivery of humanitarian assistance and support the implementation of the cessation of hostilities agreement.[51]

Traces of China's involvement in the text were apparent with, for example, insertions expressing 'grave concern regarding the threats made to oil installations, petroleum companies and their employees'. Under 'protection of civilians' clauses, China also secured agreement for the mandate to cover 'foreign nationals' and include 'active patrolling' around, among other things, 'the oil installations in particular if the Government of the Republic of South Sudan is unable or failing to provide such security'.[52]

In December 2014, in another unprecedented move, China announced it was contributing 700 combat troops (an infantry battalion) to UNMISS, to join the 350 Chinese unarmed peacekeepers already present. This has made UNMISS China's largest mission abroad. During the mandate negotiations, the UN Department of Peacekeeping Operations expressed reservations that explicitly including the protection of oil workers could impair the neutrality of the UN mission. However, China got its way, even though the Chinese troops were not stationed near South Sudan's oil fields but in Juba.[53]

Thus, China has enhanced the protection of its oil interests and citizens, working through and enhancing its involvement in the UN system. Chinese experts generally believe that remaining within the UN framework bestows international legitimacy while providing China with the opportunity to secure its own interests overseas.[54]

In for the long haul

China's special envoy to the Sudans, Zhong Jianhua, has called the situation there a 'new chapter' for Chinese foreign policy. Officially, China continues to talk of non-interference and insist that warring parties must find a solution to the conflict themselves. In reality, in its desire to protect both its nationals and its assets in the Sudans, it has become deeply involved in several rounds of conflict-resolution negotiations.

China has never before been so invested in securing a peaceful outcome in another country, and this has raised contradictions and dilemmas. Its new role as a mediator has not sat well, for example, with its status as an arms exporter. China has always denied selling arms for use in Darfur, which would be in contravention of a UN embargo.[55] However, it has conceded that it sells weapons to Khartoum for general military purposes. This has not only caused rights groups such as Amnesty International to criticise it for 'sending arms knowing that the Sudanese government is breaking the embargo';[56] it has also led Darfuri rebels to target Chinese interests and nationals inside Sudan. Similarly, the announced delivery in late 2014 of US$38m in arms from Norinco to the South Sudanese government in the middle of the civil war put into question China's neutrality as a mediator.[57]

China's experiences in Sudan fit with the growth pains of a rising great power. China is no longer a small player that can operate below the radar. In both Sudan and South Sudan, its arms contracts did not go undetected. All of this helped to burst China's initial ambitions of keeping relations with Sudan and South Sudan on a purely business footing.

China is now publicly committed to protecting its nationals and property abroad. While it would prefer to see host governments secure this, the Sudanese and South Sudanese governments' lack of capacity has forced China to seize the initiative. This has involved it in negotiating directly with rebels for the release of Chinese hostages. It has also made China more amenable to enhancing the international presence in South Sudan by contributing its own troops to the UN peacekeeping force there, and beefing up the mission's mandate to protect both civilians – including China's own – and oil installations.

China continues to institutionalise the protection of nationals abroad, and Sudan provided it the first opportunity to road-test an emergency-response mechanism in which embassies request joint work teams dispatched from Beijing.[58]

In the Sudans, a strong corporate stamp on China's foreign policy is visible and manifested through CNPC's oil interests. China has found itself embroiled in the Sudans – in much the same way that the East India Company involved the United Kingdom in India or the United Fruit Company drew the US into Central America. At this point, its ability to protect its nationals and oil interests on the ground is limited; it has had to evacuate workers instead of being capable of protecting them as they go about their jobs. This might change with the addition of Chinese peacekeepers to the revamped UNMISS force. Meanwhile, oil production in the Sudans is still running low.

Notes

1 David Smith, 'China to send 700 combat troops to South Sudan', *Guardian*, 23 December 2014. In early 2014, China sent a smaller contingent of 170 soldiers to Mali, alongside military engineers and medical staff; see Zhou Huiying, 'Helping to keep the peace in West Africa', *China Daily*, 17 November 2014.

2 It is frequently reported that China invested some £20bn in Sudan before it split in two in 2011; see, e.g., Yuwen Wu, 'China's oil fears over South Sudan fighting', BBC News, 8 January 2014. In late 2013, some 140 Chinese companies were registered in South Sudan; see Hang Zhou, 'Testing the Limits: China's Expanding Role in the South Sudanese Civil War', *China Brief* (Jamestown Foundation), vol. 14, no. 9, October 2014.

3 US Energy Information Administration (EIA), 'International Energy Statistics', accessed via http://www.eia.gov/countries/country-data.cfm?fips=SU&trk=m#pet.

4 *Ibid.*; and Yitzhak Shichor, 'Sudan: China's outpost in Africa', *China Brief* (Jamestown Foundation), vol. 5, no. 21, October 2005.

5 US Energy Information Administration (EIA), accessed at http://www.eia.gov/countries/cab.cfm?fips=su.

6 US Department of State, 'Global Patterns of Terrorism 1993', accessed at http://fas.org:8080/irp/threat/terror_93/statespon.html#Sudan.

7 CNPC, Review of 15 Years of Sino-Sudanese Petroleum Cooperation, accessed at http://www.cnpc.com.cn/en/csr2009en/201407/8fc23f51afa74701a14b3453211cb6eb/files/139ad08f4a204b79ac5cff82972e37e5.pdf.

8 Even after independence and the subsequent fall in oil production due to disagreements between Sudan and South Sudan, China received 86% of oil production from both Sudans in 2013, according to US Energy Information Administration accessed at http://www.eia.gov/countries/cab.cfm?fips=su.

9 ICC press release, 'ICC Prosecutor presents case against Sudanese President, Hassan Ahmad AL BASHIR, for genocide, crimes against humanity and war crimes

in Darfur', 14 June 2008, accessed at http://www.icc-cpi.int/en_menus/icc/situations%20and%20cases/situations/situation%20icc%200205/press%20releases/Pages/a.aspx.

10 Mathieu Duchâtel, Oliver Bräuner, Zhou Hang, 'China's Globalizing Interests, the slow shift away from non-interference', SIPRI Policy Paper No. 41, p. 31.

11 'China threatens to veto UN Darfur resolution over oil sanctions', Sudan Tribune, 18 September 2004.

12 'Darfur: UN Council imposes sanctions on four individuals, urges peace accord', UN News Centre, 25 April 2006.

13 See, e.g., Danna Harman, 'Activists press China with "Genocide Olympics" label', Christian Science Monitor, 26 June 2007.

14 Peter Schumann, 'International actors in Sudan: the Politics of Implementing Comprehensive Peace', in Sudan – No Easy Ways Out (Heinrich Boll Stiftung: Berlin, 2010), pp. 102–17.

15 Opheera McDoom, 'China's Hu tells Sudan it must solve Darfur issue', Reuters, 2 February 2007.

16 Simon Elegant, 'Beijing and the Darfur Two Step', Time, 10 May 2007.

17 'Two Chinese workers killed in Sudan', China Daily, 31 March 2004.

18 Also sometimes spelled Abu Dafra.

19 Mohamed Osman, 'Darfur Rebels Attack Oil Field, Warn Chinese to Leave', Washington Post, 26 October 2007.

20 Andrew Heavens, 'Darfur rebels vow more attack on Sudan oil fields', Reuters, 25 October 2007.

21 Arthur Bright, 'Sudanese oil field attack threatens peace talks', Christian Science Monitor, 26 October 2007.

22 Chinese official, Author interview, Beijing, August 2014.

23 See 'China's New Courtship in South Sudan', International Crisis Group, 4 April 2012; or a more detailed account in Daniel Large, 'South Sudan and China: turning enemies into friends' in Daniel Large & Luke Patey (eds) Sudan Looks East: China, India and the Politics of Asian Alternatives, (James Currey: Oxford, 2011).

24 Led by Du Yanling, director-general of the Communist Party's international department.

25 China's New Courtship in South Sudan', International Crisis Group.

26 Daniel Large, 'Between the CPA and Southern Independence: China's Post-Conflict Engagement in Sudan' in South African Institute of International Affairs. Occasional Paper no. 115, April 2012.

27 Underlining Beijing's pragmatic approach without general elections or referendums of its own; see European Council for Foreign Relations 'European Foreign Policy Scorecard 2012', p. 41, available at http://www.ecfr.eu/scorecard/2012.

28 'China's New Courtship in South Sudan', International Crisis Group.

29 US Energy Information Administration, 'Sudan and South Sudan', 3 September 2014, accessed at http://www.eia.gov/countries/cab.cfm?fips=su.

30 Nicholas Bariyo, 'South Sudan Expels Petrodar Executive', Wall Street Journal, 22 February 2012; and Machel Amos, 'South Sudan expels Petrodar boss as oil row rages', Africa Review, 22 February 2012.

31 Michael Martina, 'China's Africa envoy says South Sudan oil may flow by November', Reuters, 15 September 2012.

32 'Sudan rebels ask Beijing to pressure Khartoum', Modern Ghana, 1 February 2012.

33 Chris Buckley, 'UPDATE 2 – China says 29 workers still captive in Sudan; widespread public concern', Reuters, 30 January 2012.

34 Global Times editorial quoted in 'China Workers Abroad Becoming Easy Prey', Bloomberg, 1 February 2012.

35 Ulf Laessing and Sui-wei Lee, 'Kidnapped Chinese workers freed in Sudan oil state', Reuters, 7 February 2012.

36 Zhou Hang, 'Testing the Limits: China's Expanding Role in the South Sudanese Civil War', China Brief (Jamestown Foundation), vol. 14, no. 19, 10 October 2014.

37 'China sets up joint mechanism to provide consular protection', Xinhua, 10 February 2012.

38 MFA, Foreign Ministry Spokesperson Hua Chunying's Regular Press Conference, 24 December 2013, accessed at http://www.fmprc.gov.cn/mfa_eng/xwfw_665399/s2510_665401/2511_665403/t1111736.shtml.

39 'China to evacuate South Sudan oil workers to capital', Reuters, 20 December 2014.

40 CNPC, 'Zhongguo Shiyou nan Sudan xiangmu zhongfang renyuan shunli cheli' (CNPC Chinese staff in South Sudan successfully evacuated), 1 January 2014, accessed at http://news.cnpc.com.cn/system/2014/01/01/001465405.shtml.

41 'Nan Sudan xian zhongzu tusha baoxing waijie rao Lu'anda beiju huo chongyan' (Racial massacre in South Sudan, the international community worries the Rwanda tragedy will play out again), Global Times, 26 December 2013, accessed at 'http://world.huanqiu.com/exclusive/2013-12/4696896.html.

42 'Nan Sudan beibu ping'an ye ji zhan, Zhongguo gongmin anquan youxu cheli' (Intense war operations on a calm night in the north of South Sudan; Chinese citizens are evacuated in an orderly fashion), People's Daily, 26 December 2013, accessed at http://www.chinanews.com/hr/2013/12-26/5665183.shtml.

43 'Zhongguo fu nan Sudan weihe jingdui chenggong jiuzhu zhuanyi san ming bei kun Zhongguo gongren' (The Chinese Peacekeeping mission in South Sudan successfully saves three Chinese workers in trouble), Xinhua, 22 December 2013, accessed at http://news.xinhuanet.com/politics/2013-12/22/c_118658041.htm.

44 Zhou, 'Testing the Limits: China's Expanding Role in the South Sudanese Civil War'.

45 'South Sudan: AU, China welcome ceasefire deal', CCTV Africa, 25 January 2014, accessed at https://www.youtube.com/watch?v=vRHBHrbZuCo.

46 'Rebels slam China's conflicting roles in South Sudan', Sudan Tribune, 18 July 2014 .

47 Drazen Jorgic, 'China takes more assertive line in South Sudan diplomacy', Reuters, 5 June 2014.

48 'Rebels slam China's conflicting roles in South Sudan'.

49 'South Sudan rebel delegation heads to China', *Sudan Tribune*, 20 September 2014.

50 Mo Jingxi, 'FM defends mediation efforts in South Sudan', *China Daily*, 13 January 2015.

51 United Nations Security Council Resolution 2155 (2014), accessed at http://unscr.com/en/resolutions/2155.

52 United Nations Security Council Resolution No. 2155 (2014). See also 'Security Council adopting resolution 2155 (2014) extends mandate of mission in South Sudan, bolstering its strength to quell surging violence', 27 May 2014, accessed at http://www.un.org/News/Press/docs/2014/sc11414.doc.htm.

53 High-level Western representative to the South Sudan peace process, Author interview, September 2014; and 'China Peacekeepers in South Sudan to Focus on Protecting Civilians, UN Says', Voice of America, 15 January 2015.

54 Xue Lei, 'China's role in Sudan and South Sudan peacekeeping operations', *Global Review*, Winter 2012, pp. 12–14.

55 Although UN reports in 2005 and again in 2010 noted that Chinese weapons were found in Darfur.

56 Maggie Farley, 'China, Russia faulted for Sudan arms sales', *Los Angeles Times*, 9 May 2007.

57 lya Gridneff, 'China Halts Arms Sales to South Sudan After Norinco Shipment', Bloomberg, 30 September 2014.

58 'China sets up joint mechanism to provide consular protection', Xinhua.

CONCLUSION

What shapes foreign policy? 'Events, dear boy, events', is the answer attributed to British Prime Minister Harold Macmillan. In the past decade, there have been several defining foreign-policy events for China in which it has found itself required to protect its nationals abroad. China's global engagement has brought new challenges and subsequent adjustments to its security policies. Now a tipping point has been reached.

The need to evacuate Chinese workers from Libya in 2011 was one watershed, the murder of Chinese sailors on the Mekong was another and numerous conflict situations in Sudan provided yet more – as Beijing gradually accepted a responsibility to defend China's nationals overseas. The acceptance of this responsibility came not as part of a great-power strategy, but through China's commercial presence in weak and fragile states. The question of political risk and stability abroad has been thrust upon a China that in its foreign-policy inclinations prefers to shun involvement.

Since China's commercial and human presence is likely to continue to develop, these challenges will also grow. The gradual transformation that started in 2004 under President

Hu Jintao is only going to intensify under his successor, Xi Jinping. Xi has not only set out plans for a New Silk Road that will almost certainly increase Chinese commercial activities and the presence of Chinese workers on infrastructure projects overseas; he also confirmed at the November 2014 Chinese Communist Party Central Committee conference on foreign affairs that the protection of interests overseas had priority, and that China would 'continue to improve (its) capacity to provide such protection'.[1]

At stake is the future of China's policy of non-interference, and China's attitude towards intervention in regional and local crises. In some cases, China will not need to break with its past practice of non-interference. But other situations will entail foreign-policy experimentation. Trends suggest that China is already doing this.

The shift to a more interventionist approach

Firstly, China is entering a 'new normal' where its global economic weight and presence means its activities abroad no longer go unnoticed. Chinese nationals can no longer pass beneath the radar; they have been targeted specifically because they were Chinese in Afghanistan, Pakistan and Sudan.

The Chinese official reflex is still to rely first and foremost on host governments to protect Chinese nationals on their territory. However, there has been a noticeable change in official Chinese demands and public exhortations for other countries to carry out these protective duties. In 2011, after the deaths of Chinese sailors on the Mekong River, Premier Wen Jiabao let it be known that he had pressed Thai Prime Minister Yingluck Shinawatra to better safeguard Chinese nationals on the river. In the Sudans, it has become a Chinese diplomatic refrain to publicly demand protection and action from the host government when Chinese nationals are killed or taken hostage. One of the reasons that China's protective diplomacy is increasingly conducted in the public spotlight is clearly to placate the Chinese public, who want to see tangible actions when Chinese are threatened overseas.

Secondly, the increased commitment to protecting nationals also means that the Chinese government has to deal with kidnappings, hostages and evacuations. Having made efforts to institutionalise and centralise evacuations, the Chinese apparatus has demonstrated a capacity, particularly in Libya, to leverage sufficient resources from government, army and companies. Although China doesn't officially pay hostage ransoms, it seems to have a more flexible approach than the United States and United Kingdom. In Sudan, it has reportedly secured the release of hostages by offering another form of ransom, namely development assistance for rebel groups. This is a grey area for Chinese foreign policy, which is likely to be further tested in coming years as terrorists and other non-state groups use kidnap-for-ransom to raise revenue. Ultimately, a hostage situation may precipitate the use of military assets abroad.

Thirdly, such cases raise the issues of risk management and division of liabilities between Beijing and Chinese companies, in what some experts have labelled the 'corporatisation' of Chinese foreign policy. Most Chinese companies investing or working abroad are state-owned enterprises and thus part of the Communist Party system of control, but they have nevertheless shown a commercial willingness to take great risks. The Chinese government apparatus, by contrast, is inherently risk-averse. Therefore when trouble strikes, is it the responsibility of the individual companies or of the Chinese government, which also ultimately owns them, to safeguard assets and workers? Chinese companies with their appetite for high risk in fragile states are pulling the risk-averse Chinese government into new areas of insecurity and conflict.

China's position as an arms exporter has sometimes caused difficulties for Chinese firms in specific countries. When China was a smaller economy and had less global exposure, it was easier for it to avoid criticism over arms sales to controversial customers. That has changed. In Sudan, arms sales by state-owned Norinco led to attacks on Chinese nationals and made it harder for China to be trusted as an honest mediator, or even just as a neutral business partner supporting the country's economic development. In Libya, mere talks about arms sales to the embattled Gadhafi regime led the rebels who formed the new government to mistrust Beijing.

Beijing's traditional, hands-off approach meant it treated the official government as its sole interlocutor in any given country.[2] However, the Chinese government is learning to engage with rebels and opposition groups. Although it was late to recognise the new authorities in Libya, Beijing found it necessary to reach out to the National Transitional Council as it moved from opposition to government. When Syria descended into civil war in 2011, China was more nimble in reaching out to the Syrian opposition, even while maintaining formal ties with the government of President Bashar al-Assad. As Chinese government adviser and expert Shi Yinhong told us about China's involvement in Libya in 2011: 'In 1979, China lost on dealing purely with the Shah in Iran, in 1989 on dealing only with Ceausescu's Romania until his rule crumbled, and in 1999 with Milosevic's Serbia. Now, China has got to be smarter.'[3]

Such a 'smarter' approach is evident in the complicated world of Pakistani and Afghan politics, where China has communicated directly even with Islamist groups and political parties such as the Taliban and Jamaat-e-Islami. More surprisingly, given its own hard line on internal separatism, China made early overtures to the leaders of South Sudan's independence movement – and later supported the independence referendum, including by fielding a Chinese observation team.

This demonstrates that Beijing is becoming more engaged, albeit in its own particular manner. It is also employing more proactive diplomacy in high-risk countries where it has interests. In both Sudan and in Afghanistan/Pakistan, Chinese diplomacy broke new ground by nominating special envoys to focus on the region. China has also taken steps towards international mediation. In the Mekong River murder case, it was China who summoned the other riparian powers to a summit in Beijing to discuss the future protection of trade and Chinese nationals in the region. In the 'Heart of Asia' conference process on Afghanistan, China has gone from being a lukewarm observer to hosting the 2014 round, as well as putting itself forward as mediator in the Afghan reconciliation process.

China's comprehension of the underlying causes of instability appears to be evolving. Promoting development in South Sudan, for example, is a difficult task for any country or organisation involved, but China has tried to do this by building much-needed infrastructure for the impoverished new nation. Having begun maritime patrols in the Gulf of Aden alongside other international task forces, China also funded development and humanitarian projects in Somalia, whose poverty was the root cause of the piracy problem off its coast.[4]

Clearly, China can be persuaded to discuss and care about the plight of fragile states through a stability and risk perspective. China will not share some Western countries' ambitions of promoting democracy around the world, but there could be common ground in working on stability and sound economic governance. Many in Beijing now realise that placing all their bets with one strong authoritarian ruler might no longer be sufficient to protect long-term Chinese interests in that country.

China's commitment to protecting its nationals overseas has given some of its strongest domestic agencies, particularly the Ministry of Public Security (MPS), a role in foreign policy. In the Mekong River case, the MPS demonstrated its clout overseas by liaising with law enforcement in neighbouring countries to capture the Chinese sailors' killers and, in an unprecedented extraterritorial trial, bring them to justice in China. Plans to launch a drone strike in Myanmar, although swiftly abandoned, showed that at least some in the MPS are ready to challenge known boundaries and non-interference. Increasing global terrorism, sometimes specifically directed against Chinese nationals and interests, will only expand the MPS's overseas activities, as already evident in its interest in Pakistan and Afghanistan.

Incremental military involvement in the evacuations of Chinese working or living in crisis-hit countries makes it clear that there will be little hesitation in Beijing in deploying naval, air-force or special-forces personnel when Chinese lives are at risk and charter flights do not provide adequate guarantees. These evacuations also provide the military with an opportunity to demonstrate their capabilities. Force projection in large non-combatant evacuations is likely in future following the Libyan and Yemeni precedents.

The next time trouble erupts in a fragile state and endangers Chinese interests, there will certainly be a greater push from Chinese companies and citizens for the Chinese authorities to act decisively. When, where and under which extreme circumstances this will happen is an open question, as is the degree of military involvement. Protecting nationals overseas could also eventually entail more clear-cut breaks with current foreign-policy practices, especially if evacuation proves to be an insufficient solution.

China's changing global risk map also has an impact on the country's approach to international conflict resolution. In the

United Nations Security Council (UNSC), China acquiesced to action in support of the anti-Gadhafi uprising because, among other reasons, it had nationals and business interests to secure in Libya. In Syria, with fewer nationals and assets to secure, China reverted to its classical doctrine of non-interference in other states' internal affairs.

Where the Chinese presence – either corporate or human – has reached a critical mass, China is looking pragmatically at international conflict resolution. After its initial reluctance to comment on the conflict in Sudan's Darfur region, China ended up using its close links to the regime in Khartoum to push for an UN-mandated peacekeeping force. In South Sudan, China has contributed combat troops to the UN Mission in South Sudan peacekeeping force after managing in 2014 to weave the protection of its own oil interests into the mission's extended mandate.

Whenever the UNSC backs peacekeeping, China will be able to shape the international community's response and continue making greater contributions to peacekeeping missions. There is no reason for China to change its current preference for multilateral solutions within the UN system; this is China's natural choice and simply the best policy in terms of cost and legitimacy. In the same vein, China talked about its 'international humanitarianism' when taking additional responsibility for rescuing foreign nationals in Yemen. This gives China's increasingly global military presence a benign appearance.

More generally, a lesson of China's ongoing policy change is that the West should cooperate with China, not on the basis of grand and abstract principles of democracy and human rights but on concrete cases where there is a convergence of interests in stability. This in turn could have an impact on China's long-term calculations.

What lies ahead on China's great-power trajectory?

Most China watchers were surprised by Beijing's decision to send frigates abroad as part of international anti-piracy efforts in the Gulf of Aden in 2008. After its evacuation of nearly 36,000 nationals from Libya in 2011, including via Il-76 air-force transportation aircraft, the world glimpsed the scale of the Chinese human presence in Africa and the lengths to which Beijing was willing to go to save Chinese lives. Western experts noted the expansion of Chinese peacekeeping contributions as a welcome support to international security, but it was only in 2014 that China agreed to send combat troops to join such a mission – breaking what was long considered to have been a taboo. Before it dispatched a 700-strong infantry battalion to South Sudan in early 2015, China persuaded others in the UN Security Council to expand the mandate of the UNMISS peacekeeping force to include protecting foreign oil workers, most of whom are Chinese.

How far can China continue on this path in future? What will be the impact on international security? There are many possible scenarios. Some of these postulate Chinese unilateral action and greater military involvement; some of them assume unprecedented foreign-policy adjustments. Still others could lead to greater cooperation with the West on safeguarding stability in fragile states.

With Chinese citizens at risk when unmanageable civil conflict erupts abroad, China is more likely to lend stronger support for multilateral interventions if its own interests are at stake. If, for example, Angola – with its more than 200,000 Chinese nationals, huge Chinese investments and loans – were hit by internal strife, China could suddenly be the permanent Security Council member clamouring for an international response. This might not exactly transform Beijing into the 'responsible stakeholder' in the international order coveted by

US policymakers. Nonetheless, with its massive rescue operation in Libya and its attempts to mediate in Sudan and South Sudan, China has revealed itself to be willing to accept responsibility abroad – especially when the situation impinges on its citizens' interests.

China is not the first country compelled to send special envoys, police or military personnel abroad to safeguard the activities of expanding national companies. In the nineteenth century, the commercial adventures of the East India Company compelled the British state to intervene in China, sparking the Opium Wars. Just as the United States built the Panama Canal in 1914 as it tiptoed towards great-power status, a Chinese company is now aiming to build a super-sized canal through Nicaragua to be completed by 2020 – at an estimated cost of US\$49 billion. And just as involvement in Panama presented the US with sensitive foreign-policy questions, including ownership of the area and the rights of local inhabitants, Chinese construction in Nicaragua could well create challenges beyond the financial costs of the operation.

In 1850, Britain's foreign secretary, Lord Palmerston, ordered the British navy into the Aegean Sea to protect a British subject, Don Pacifico, and reclaim his lost property. Palmerston compared British subjects to citizens of ancient Rome, who could proudly assert their rights by announcing 'Civis Romanus sum' (I am a Roman citizen). According to Palmerston, 'a British subject, in whatever land he may be, shall feel confident that the watchful eye and the strong arm of England will protect him from injustice and wrong'.

Politicians' promises to protect fellow nationals abroad have an ominous ring following the annexation of Crimea in March 2014, and President Vladimir Putin's subsequent promise to 'actively defend the rights of Russians, our compatriots abroad, using the entire range of available means – from political and economic to operations under international humanitarian law and the right of self-defence'.[5] If China were to likewise extend a protective umbrella to overseas Chinese, with millions scattered in Myanmar, Vietnam, Singapore, Malaysia, Philippines and Indonesia, it would cause much greater consternation among its neighbours than it has with its current maritime behaviour and disputes.

Even with Beijing's currently more restrained interpretation of 'nationals abroad', the move to protect them across the globe is gradually leading to a twenty-first-century version of Palmerston's Roman dictum, namely 'Civis Sinicus Sum' (I am a Chinese citizen).[6] The magnetic pull of these interests will be a defining trait of Chinese foreign policy in coming years.

Notes

[1] 'Xi eyes more enabling international environment for China's peaceful development', Xinhua, 30 November 2014.

[2] In this regard, China's non-interference policy is actually not that old. One of the many slogans of the Mao era was 'to rebel is justified' and China supported communist revolutionary movements around the world with training camps and military support. This support of rebels dwindled in the mid-1970s and revolutionary movements paying tribute to China's revolutionary past, such as the Maoists in Nepal, are now more a source of embarrassment than anything else; see Jonas Parello-Plesner, 'China's Libya Hedge Highlights Shift on Noninterference', *World Politics Review*, 14 June 2011.

[3] Shi Yinhong, Author interview, Beijing, April 2011.

[4] From 2000 to 2011, there were seven instances of China providing development assistance to Somalia; see Austin Strange, Bradley Parks, Michael J. Tierney, Andreas Fuchs, Axel Dreher and Vijaya Ramachandran, 'China's Development Finance to Africa: A Media-Based Approach to Data Collection', Center for Global Development (CGD) Working Paper, no. 323, April 2013, accessed at http://www10.iadb.org/intal/intalcdi/PE/2013/12317.pdf. In 2013, Beijing agreed to reconstruct Mogadishu stadium, the national theatre and the Galkayo–Burao Road; see China Aid Data, accessed at http://china.aiddata.org/projects/.

[5] President of Russia, Speech to the Conference of Russian ambassadors and permanent representatives, 1 July 2014, accessed at http://en.kremlin.ru/events/president/news/46131.

6   Jonas Parello-Plesner, 'Civis Sinicus Sum: China's Great Power Burdens in Libya', *World Politics Review*, 3 March 2011.

INDEX